D0711318

PROFESSOR ARTHUR S. LINK was born in New Market, Virginia, and studied at the University of North Carolina. He is the author of *American Epoch, Woodrow Wilson and the Progressive Era,* and the monumental biography of Wilson, of which five volumes have been published to date. He is at present Professor of History and Director of the Woodrow Wilson Papers at Princeton University.

WILSON *the Diplomatist*

WILSON *the Diplomatist*

A LOOK AT HIS MAJOR

FOREIGN POLICIES

Arthur S. Link

NEW VIEWPOINTS

A Division of Franklin Watts, Inc.

New York/1974

WILSON THE DIPLOMATIST. Copyright © 1957 by The
Johns Hopkins Press. This book was originally published in 1957 by The Johns Hopkins Press, Baltimore,
and is here reprinted by arrangement.

First NEW VIEWPOINTS edition published 1974 by
Franklin Watts, Inc.

Manufactured in the United States of America.

Library of Congress Catalog Card Number: 74-10183
Standard Book Number: 531-06461-1 (pbk.)

PREFACE

THE FIVE CHAPTERS that make up this book were presented substantially in their present printed form as the Albert Shaw Lectures on Diplomatic History at The Johns Hopkins University from December 3 to 7, 1956.

In thinking about what I should attempt to do in the time that I had at my disposal, it seemed obvious that I could not prepare a summary account of Woodrow Wilson's foreign policies without saying what was already entirely familiar and without also repeating what I myself had already written in part. Thus I tried as much as possible to minimize the narrative and descriptive portions and to spend most of my time on analysis and interpretation. My technique throughout was to ask, and to try to answer, what seemed to me to be the most important questions about Wilson the diplomatist and some of his major foreign policies and programs.

In the first chapter (or lecture) I endeavored to analyze the ideals, assumptions, and ambitions that shaped Wilson's actions in the field of foreign affairs, his methods of forming conclusions and policies, and his techniques as a diplomatist. The second and third chapters I devoted to some large and still unresolved questions about Wilson's policies of neutrality and the causes of American participation in the First World War—for example: What did Wilson really think about the issues involved in the European war? Why did he accept the British maritime system and resist the German submarine challenge? What were the pressures that molded his policies of neutrality? Why did Wilson decide to go to war against Germany in 1917, instead of maintaining an armed neutrality, as he presumably might have done? In the fourth chapter I attempted to analyze the development of Wilson's thinking about a peace settlement, and I surveyed his work at Paris with the objective of determining the degree to which he succeeded or failed in accomplishing his peace ideals. The final chapter represents an effort to summarize Wilson's thinking about the League and collective security (a matter largely ignored by historians), and to highlight what I thought were the really important issues in the great debate over ratification of the Treaty of Versailles.

It will soon become evident to the reader that I have not covered all of Wilson's foreign policies and programs. It was not possible to cover the whole ground within the limitations of the lecture series, and I did not think that it was desirable to try to do so in this book. My purpose was limited to an analysis of Wilson's policies toward Europe and the problem of world organization, and I never meant to cover everything.

Looking back over these lectures, I can see that concentration upon analysis and interpretation has led me at times to make some evaluations of my own. If this is true, I trust that I have always remembered my own limitations, that I have not been Olympian in judgment, and that I have been able to add some insight toward understanding a complex and great man. It has not been my purpose either to praise or to condemn, but if the over-all assessment of Wilson's record in the field of foreign affairs is an impressively favorable one, as I think it is, then that is a tribute to the President's steadfastness, idealism, courage, and ability to see things in their long-run perspective.

Students and specialists who read this book will perhaps want a word of explanation about the lack of any elaborate scholarly apparatus. These lectures consist largely of interpretations and analyses derived from many years of research and reading about Wilson and his time. It would be an endless process to attempt to footnote every generalization, and it would, worse still, obscure my very purpose in writing this book. I have, therefore, included footnotes only for the purpose of citing the reference of a quotation, acknowledging my obligation to certain secondary works, and calling the reader's attention to some of the best recent work in the field.

Writing this Preface gives me an opportunity to express my thanks to Professor C. Vann Woodward and the other members of the Shaw Lecture Committee for inviting me to give these lectures during the Wilson Centennial, and to Professor Woodward and his colleagues in the History Department at The Johns Hopkins University for their warm hospitality while I was on their campus. They all helped make giving these lectures a memorable experience.

My colleagues in the History Department at Northwestern University, Professor Franklin D. Scott and Richard W. Leopold; my good friend, Professor Samuel Flagg Bemis of Yale University; and my wife, Margaret Douglas Link, have all read this manuscript with an almost loving care. They are not in any sense responsible for the errors that may remain, and they have made a far larger contribution than they will ever know.

I have dedicated this book to my former professors at the University of North Carolina and Columbia University, Fletcher M. Green, Howard K. Beale, and Henry Steele Commager. Along with the dedication goes my affectionate tribute to them as teachers and scholars.

Arthur S. Link

Evanston, Illinois
March 29, 1957

PREFACE TO THE SECOND EDITION

The occasion of the second printing of *Wilson the Diplomatist* affords me an opportunity to say a few words by way of amendment of the original text. I wrote this book six years ago. I do not believe that I would change it fundamentally in organization or scope if I were writing it today. But I would alter emphases, interpretations, and details, among others, in the following ways:

First. I would give greater emphasis to Wilson's very rapid and striking progress toward mastery of the techniques of diplomacy gained from day-to-day experience, accompanied by an even more important growth in wisdom. The first chapter concentrates too much on the Wilson of the first two years of his presidency, which was the time of his apprenticeship as a diplomatist. He learned many useful things quickly. Experience in dealing with Mexico, to cite one example, taught him some of the natural limits of the use of force in attempting to obtain domestic change in other countries, and his Mexican policy from 1915 to 1917 was very different from his policy from 1913 to 1914. This experience also had an obvious impact on his later attitudes toward the possibilities of intervention in Russia.

Second. I would certainly rewrite pages 22–27 wherein I comment on Wilson's egotism in conducting foreign affairs and his relations, specifically, with Lansing and Walter Page. A more accurate statement would be that Wilson sought and valued all kinds of advice and reserved final decision to himself because he believed that he alone bore responsibility to the American people and history, and that conflict between the President and his advisers occurred only when the latter were unwilling to accept Wilson's ultimate decisions. Moreover, as I have shown in the forthcoming fourth volume of my biography, it is inaccurate to say, as I did on page 26, that Lansing was " completely loyal to the President." Neither were Page and House, for that matter. There were times, for example, the occasion of Wilson's great peace effort in 1916–1917, when all or some of the President's intimate advisers were working undercover to defeat his aims. Thus I would want to add the further comment that Wilson often had to work toward his objectives in foreign policy under the severe handicap of occasional disloyalty among his closest associates.

Third. Recent research on the armed ship controversy of 1916–1917 has led me to conclude that the statement on page 47 that Wilson and Lansing reversed their policy toward armed ships in February, 1916, is misleading. The two men, while abandoning Lansing's proposal for disarming of merchant ships, also sought to find a formula that would be technically neutral without running much risk of conflict with Germany over submarine attacks against armed merchantmen. They succeeded, and the issue was never a serious one in German-American relations. In this connection, I would want to rewrite two brief passages—the statement on page 58 that the German *Sussex* pledge covered armed ships, and the one on page 80 that the German proclamation of unlimited submarine warfare against armed merchantmen, dated January 10, 1917, was a technical violation of the Sussex pledge. These are egregiously in error. Wilson was able to obtain the *Sussex* pledge precisely because he did not force the armed ship issue with Germany.

Fourth. I would not change many words in my analysis (pages 62–67) of the reasons for British refusal to permit Wilson's mediation under the House-Grey Memorandum. I would, however, now be able to say that new evidence reveals that Sir Edward Grey and other British leaders never took the House-Grey Memorandum seriously, not even when it was initialed.

Fifth. I think that my analysis (pages 73–81) of German motivation in launching the all-out submarine campaign in 1917 is sound as far as it goes. But if I were writing these pages today, I would be much less certain that hope of a smashing victory was the only reason for the fateful decision made at Pless Castle on January 9, 1917. Additional work in German sources has persuaded me that the decision was born not only of hope but also of desperate despair occasioned by the Allied rebuff of the German peace offer and the conviction that Germany inevitably would lose the war if she could not obtain some decision in 1917. I must add that I think that I was unfair to Chancellor Bethmann-Hollweg on page 79. He had literally exhausted himself in keeping military and naval chieftains in rein all through 1916. Events were simply out of his control in 1917, and it is difficult to see how he could have made any decision at Pless on January 9, 1917, other than to yield.

Sixth. I would rewrite certain sentences in my analysis (pages 81–90) of the reasons why Wilson concluded that the United States had no alternative but to accept the status of a belligerent in 1917. Among the three ships mentioned on page 86, only the *Illinois* and *Vigilancia* were sunk without warning; the *City of Memphis* was destroyed after warning and evacuation of crew. I think that it is very doubtful that Wilson, as I said on page 88, was influenced by the fear that the Central Powers were about to win the war on account of the submarine campaign. There is no evidence that anyone in Washington knew the desperate nature of the Allied situation, or that Wilson was importantly motivated by considerations of national security in his own decision for war. If I were writing these pages now, I would give much greater emphasis than I did in the original text to Wilson's conviction that the war was in its final stages, American belligerency would have the effect of shortening, not prolonging, the war, and belligerency had the one advantage of guaranteeing him an important role in peacemaking. I have a rather full discussion of these points in my fourth volume.

Seventh. I would want to revise my picture of Wilson after his return from Paris in 1919 (pages 130–133). I think that the present text emphasizes too much his rigidity and refusal to discuss the Versailles Treaty and does not take sufficient note of his serious efforts to win moderate Republican support. If I were writing this passage today, I do not believe that I would use the quotation on page 131 attributed to Wilson by Ambassador Jusserand. I think that I understand what Wilson meant, as he later made a reference to taking one's medicine. But the quotation as it now stands gives an inaccurate impression.

Eighth. I would want, finally, to rewrite pages 153–156, in which I analyze the reasons for Wilson's refusal to accept the Lodge reservations in order to obtain the Senate's consent to ratification of the Versailles Treaty. I would now give much greater emphasis to Wilson's conviction, so strikingly and poignantly revealed in Admiral Grayson's little memoir, that he could not co-operate in a course of action that violated his sacred pledges to the American people and the world; that it would be better for the United States to stay out of the League of Nations than to go into it without purpose and determination to enforce the Covenant; and that he had to hold fast to what he thought was right in the faith that the event and outcome were in the hands of God.

Arthur S. Link

Princeton, New Jersey
September 14, 1963

CONTENTS

WILSON *the Diplomatist*

CHAPTER I

WILSON *the diplomatist*

A GAUNT MAN of serious mien walked to the stands outside the east front of the Capitol on Tuesday, March 4, 1913, to take the oath as twenty-eighth president of the United States. He was Woodrow Wilson, born in Staunton, Virginia, on December 28, 1856, educated at Davidson College and Princeton University, trained in law at the University of Virginia, and prepared for a career in teaching and scholarship in history and political science at The Johns Hopkins University. From 1885 to 1902 he had taught in succession at Bryn Mawr College, Wesleyan University in Connecticut, The Johns Hopkins University, and Princeton University. Elevated to the presidency of Princeton in 1902, he had helped to transform that venerable college into a university of distinction. Embroiled in a personal controversy with the Dean of the Graduate School, he had escaped the troubled Princeton scene by accepting nomination for the governorship of New Jersey in the summer of 1910. Elected governor, he had gone on with irresistible momentum to capture the Democratic presidential nomination and the presidency itself in 1912.

The man who was inaugurated on that March morning in 1913 was privileged to guide the destinies of the United States during eight of the most critical years of the modern epoch. For the American people, the period 1913 to 1921 was a time at home of far-reaching attempts to confront and resolve the dilemma posed by the existence of private economic autocracy in a political and social democracy. Abroad, it was a time of revolutionary upheaval in countries near and far, of cataclysmic world war, and of portentous shifts in the balance of power that threatened to crumble the foundations of the international community.

As a domestic leader, articulating American democratic ideals and utilizing the resources of party and presidential leadership to devise and achieve solutions for the problems raised by twentieth-century economic developments, Wilson succeeded so well that he earned an undisputed place among the first rank of presidents. As a leader in foreign affairs, guiding the American people from provincialism toward world leadership and responsibilities, Wilson's contribution was even more significant for the long future than were his immediate achievements in domestic affairs. The sources of his strength and weakness as a maker of foreign policy will perhaps become evident, both implicitly and explicitly, as we proceed in these lectures.

There is considerable revelation in the nature of Wilson's training as a diplomatist, which was, insofar as it went, exclusively theoretical. Few men have come to the White House better equipped in the philosophy or more adequately trained in the techniques of domestic leadership than Woodrow Wilson. He is saved from the reverse generalization—that few men have ever begun the presidency with less experience and training in the field of foreign affairs than he had had—only because of the naïveté of most beginners in the White House in this

field. " It would be the irony of fate if my administration
had to deal chiefly with foreign affairs," Wilson remarked
to a Princeton friend a few days before he went to Washington in 1913. It was a frank acknowledgement of the
fact that, as a scholar and analyst, he had been almost
exclusively concerned with domestic politics in the Anglo-
American tradition and interested only casually in the
mechanisms and history of foreign relations.

To be sure, in the late nineteenth century, when Wilson
did most of his scholarly writing, the average American
was caught up in great political and economic movements
at home and knew next to nothing about affairs abroad.
But Wilson was not an average American; he was a distinguished writer and teacher in the fields of government,
history, and international law. Yet at least before the
turn of the century he wrote and spoke almost as if foreign
policy were a minor concern of great powers.

In his first book, *Congressional Government*, an inquiry
into the practical functioning of the federal government
published in 1885, Wilson made only a passing reference
to foreign affairs, and that in connection with the Senate's
treaty-making power.[1] Four years later Wilson published
The State, an excellent pioneer text in comparative government. Out of a total of more than one hundred pages
devoted to the development of law and legal institutions,
he gave a page and a half to international law. In his
analysis of the administrative structures of modern governments, he described the machinery of the foreign relations of the British Empire in five words, but devoted
twenty-six pages to local government in England; and he
gave thirteen times as much space to the work of the In-
terior Department as to the Department of State in the
American government. Finally, in his summary chapters

---

[1] *Congressional Government, A Study in American Politics* (Boston and
New York, 1885), pp. 232-34.

on the functions and objects of government, he put foreign relations at the bottom of his list of what he called the " constituent functions " and then went on to elaborate the functions and objects of government without even mentioning the conduct of external affairs! [2]

Wilson began to evince more than a casual interest in foreign affairs for the first time in the late 1890's and early 1900's. In part he was reacting to disturbing new shifts in international power and in American thinking about the future role of the United States in the world as a consequence of the Venezuelan controversy, the war with Spain, the extension of American interests to the Far East, and the acquisition of an overseas empire. Thus Wilson approved President Cleveland's assertion, made during the Venezuelan boundary dispute with Great Britain, of the right of the United States to compel a European state to arbitrate a territorial controversy anywhere in the Western Hemisphere.[3] After some earlier doubts about the wisdom of the war with Spain and of acquiring overseas possessions, he concluded that the war was the natural outgrowth of American industrial might and that it was America's duty to retain the Philippines and teach the Filipinos order and self-government, even if the effort required the use of force.[4] To cite a final example, he echoed the propaganda of imperialists like Alfred T. Mahan and Albert J. Beveridge in declaring that the flag must follow trade and that the United States must acquire colonies and markets abroad.[5]

Wilson, however, did more than merely react to the epochal developments at home and abroad around the

---

[2] *The State, Elements of Historical and Practical Politics* (Boston, 1889), *passim.*

[3] " Mr. Cleveland as President," *Atlantic Monthly*, LXXIX (March, 1897), 298.

[4] " The Ideals of America," *ibid.*, XC (December, 1902), 727-30.

[5] *History of the American People* (5 vols.; New York, 1902), V, 296.

turn of the century; he also thought seriously about their future impact upon American policies and institutions. The war with Spain, he asserted with growing conviction, had been only one sign of a more important underlying development—the end of American isolation and the inevitable beginning of a new era in which the United States would have to play an ever-widening role in world politics. "Of a sudden, as it seemed, and without premeditation," he wrote in the concluding pages of his *History of the American People,*

> the United States had turned away from their long-time, deliberate absorption in their own domestic development, from the policy professed by every generation of their statesmen from the first, of separation from the embarrassing entanglements of foreign affairs; had given themselves a colonial empire, and taken their place of power in the field of international politics. No one who justly studied the courses of their life could reasonably wonder at the thing that had happened. . . . A quick instinct apprised American statesmen that they had come to a turning point in the progress of the nation, which would have disclosed itself in some other way if not in this, had the war for Cuba not made it plain. It had turned from developing its own resources to make conquest of the markets of the world.[6]

It followed inexorably, Wilson added in a revealing essay in 1901, that Americans were living in a new and more perilous age, in which changed circumstances had rendered meaningless and dangerous the time-honored traditions of self-sufficiency and of security through isolation. "There is no masking or concealing the new order of the world," he warned. "It is not the world of the eighteenth century, nor yet of the nineteenth." There were radically new forces at work which would determine the

[6] *Ibid.,* pp. 294-96.

future of mankind; there were shifts in the balance of power that portended new rivalries and threatened the peace. The American people, he concluded, were now neighbors to the world, whether they liked it or not; they could not escape the coming challenges by ignoring them; they had, perforce, to devise new foreign policies and to become efficient in executing them.[7]

Wilson also saw clearly that the sudden emergence of the United States to world power would have a profound and enduring impact upon the location of authority and the system of leadership in the federal government. " Much the most important change to be noticed," he wrote in the preface to the fifteenth edition of *Congressional Government* in 1900,

> is the result of the war with Spain upon the lodgment and exercise of power within our federal system: the greatly increased power and opportunity for construc- tive statesmanship given the President, by the plunge into international politics and into the administration of distant dependencies, which has been that war's most striking and momentous consequence.[8]

" The war with Spain again changed the balance of parts," Wilson asserted in 1907.

> Foreign questions became leading questions again, as they had been in the first days of the government, and in them the President was of necessity leader. Our new place in the affairs of the world has since that year of transformation kept him at the front of our govern- ment, where our own thoughts and the attention of men everywhere is centred upon him. . . . The President can

---

[7] " Democracy and Efficiency," *Atlantic Monthly,* LXXXVII (March, 1901), 292.

[8] *Congressional Government* (15th ed.; Boston and New York, 1900 [?]), p. xi.

never again be the mere domestic figure he has been throughout so large a part of our history. The nation has risen to the first rank in power and resources. . . . Our President must always, henceforth, be one of the great powers of the world, whether he act greatly and wisely or not. . . . We have but begun to see the presidential office in this light; but it is the light which will more and more beat upon it, and more and more determine its character and its effect upon the politics of the nation.[9]

There is the temptation to conclude from this analysis of Wilson's observations during the decade 1898-1907 that, as one authority has said, he had demonstrated an understanding of the foreign relations of his country and considerable preparation for their conduct by the time he entered the White House.[10] Much, of course, depends upon the criteria that one applies. Compared to a Grant or a Harding, Wilson does indeed seem an eminent authority. On the other hand, to compare Wilson with a Jefferson or a John Quincy Adams is to point up some of the deficiencies in the latter-day President's intellectual and practical training for the difficult business of managing the foreign affairs of a great power.

The strengths and weaknesses in Wilson's unconscious preparation as a diplomatist will, I trust, become more fully evident as we proceed in this analysis, but it might be well to summarize them at this point. There was to his advantage the fact that he had done much serious thinking about general principles of politics and national ideals that transcended geographical boundaries. That is to say, Wilson came to the presidency equipped with a coherent and

[9] *Constitutional Government in the United States* (New York, 1908), pp. 59, 78.
[10] Harley Notter, *The Origins of the Foreign Policy of Woodrow Wilson* (Baltimore, 1937), p. 145.

deeply rooted philosophy about the nature and ends of
government, a philosophy that could be readily translated
into the basis of a foreign policy. Also to his advantage
was the fact of his awareness of the larger dimensions of
the diplomatic revolution of the period and the impact of
that revolution upon American political institutions.

Balanced on the debit side were certain obvious deficiencies in Wilson's thought and training in foreign afffairs.
The most serious of these was his failure before 1913 to
do any systematic thinking about the nature, complexity,
and difficulties of foreign policy and his assumption that
the main task of diplomacy was the simple one of trans-
lating national ideals into a larger program of action.

Secondly, there was Wilson's apparent ignorance of or
unconcern with the elementary facts about the main
thrusts of American diplomacy from 1901 to 1913 and
about the tensions that were impelling Europe toward a
general war during the same period. Even about those
events on the international scene in which he evidenced a
keen interest, the war with Spain and its immediate
aftermath, much of Wilson's thinking was superficial and
reflected more the faddish thought of the time than an
astute understanding of what was taking place. Indeed,
after the thrill of the war and of empire had quickly
passed, Wilson apparently lost virtually all interest in
affairs abroad. There were tremendous new developments
in American foreign policy and furious partisan debates
at home between 1901 and 1913. There were recurrent
crises in Europe during the prolonged prelude to the war
that would break out in 1914. Yet throughout this period,
during which Wilson emerged as a pre-eminent political
leader, he spoke and acted as if foreign problems did not
exist. For example, during a brilliant campaign for the
Democratic presidential nomination and for the presidency

from 1911 to 1912, he never once mentioned a foreign issue that was not primarily a domestic concern.

A good argument can be made to the effect that Wilson was so absorbed in plans for Princeton from 1902 to 1910 and so engrossed in his political apprenticeship from 1910 to 1913 that he had neither time nor energy for a serious study of foreign policy. The argument has some merit, but we must also conclude that Wilson did not concern himself seriously with affairs abroad during the period 1901 to 1913 both because he was not interested and because he did not think that they were important enough to warrant any diversion from the mainstream of his thought. Therefore, Wilson was not being unduly self-deprecatory when he remarked before he went to Washington how ironical it would be if his administration had to deal chiefly with foreign affairs. He was simply recognizing the obvious fact of his primary concern with domestic issues and his superior training for leadership in solving them.

Regardless of the adequacy or inadequacy of his preparation, Wilson after 1913 faced foreign problems of greater magnitude than any president had confronted since the early years of the nineteenth century. Whether he responded wisely or unwisely to the mounting international challenges of the years from 1913 to 1920, he executed policies that were on the whole firmly grounded upon a consistent body of principles and assumptions that supplied motive power and shaped and governed policy in the fields of action. These principles and assumptions were deeply rooted in Wilson's general thinking before 1913 about cosmology, ethics, the nature and ends of government, and the role of his own country in the creative development of mankind; they were in turn enlarged and refined as Wilson sought to apply them in

practical affairs after his inauguration. Determining and
controlling, they gave both strength and weakness to the
diplomatist in action.

The foundations of all of Wilson's political thinking
were the religious and ethical beliefs and values that he
inherited from the Christian tradition and from his own
Presbyterian theology. In matters of basic Christian
faith, Wilson was like a little child, never doubting, always
believing, and drawing spiritual sustenance from Bible
reading, church attendance, and prayer. Having derived
his beliefs from the Shorter Catechism, his father's ser-
mons, and the Presbyterian scholastics, Wilson was Calvin-
istic in theology. He believed in a sovereign God, just
and stern as well as loving; in a moral universe, the laws
of which ruled nations as well as men; in the supreme
revelation and redemption of Jesus Christ; and in the Bible
as the incomparable word of God and the rule of life. He
was a predestinarian, not so much in his apparent belief
in election as in his conviction that God controlled history
and used men and nations in the unfolding of His plan
according to His purposes. Few ministers of the gospel
gave more eloquent voice to these beliefs than did Wilson
in his day; to point out that there was nothing unique
about them is not to detract from their underlying and
pervasive importance.[11]

From such spiritual roots grew a sturdy tree of character, integrity, and concern for first principles in political
action—in brief, all the components of the idealism that
was the unifying force in Wilson's life. In the conduct of

---

[11] For examples of Wilson's religious addresses and writings, see " The
Ministry and the Individual " and " The Bible and Progress," printed in
Ray S. Baker and William E. Dodd (eds.), *The Public Papers of Woodrow
Wilson, College and State* (2 vols.; New York, 1925), II, 178-87, 291-302; for a
description and analysis, see Arthur S. Link, *Wilson: The New Freedom*
(Princeton, N. J., 1956), pp. 64-65.

foreign affairs this idealism meant for him the subordination of immediate goals and material interests to superior ethical standards and the exaltation of moral and spiritual purposes. This is not to say that he ignored the existence and powerful operation of economic forces in international life. Indeed, for a brief period following the Spanish-American War he seemed almost to verge upon an economic determinism in his analysis of developments, both past and present, upon the international scene. As president, moreover, he was not unmindful of the necessities of a viable international economic life, of the material interests of Americans abroad, or of the economic rivalries that helped to produce conflict among nations. Even so, idealism was the main drive of Wilson's thinking about international relations. As he put it, foreign policy must not be defined in " terms of material interest," but should be "more concerned about human rights than about property rights." [12]

A second main theme in Wilson's political thinking with large consequences for his foreign policy was his belief in democracy as the most humane and Christian form of government. From the beginning to the end of his adult career he studied, wrote about, and put into practice the essential aspects of democratic government, and it would be superfluous here to review his splendid synthesis of the Anglo-American democratic theories and traditions. More important for our purposes is an understanding of the way in which these assumptions helped to form his objectives and to determine his actions in the field of foreign affairs.

Much, of course, depended upon Wilson's view of the nature and capacities of man. There is in his thinking an

---

[12] For a rewarding amplification of the foregoing generalizations, see William Diamond, *The Economic Thought of Woodrow Wilson* (Baltimore, 1943), pp. 131-61.

implicit if never an outright repudiation of the classical Presbyterian emphasis upon original sin, and a strong strain of nineteenth-century Christian optimism and social Darwinism. To be sure, he never completely lost sight of man's capacity for evil, but he seems often to have forgotten it, so strong was his faith in man's inherent goodness and in the possibility of progress.

These were the controlling assumptions. It followed in Wilson's mind that all people were capable of self-government because all were endowed with inherent character and a capacity for growth. He was no visionary in these beliefs; following his master Burke, he repudiated and condemned utopianism and taught that people learned democracy only by long years of disciplined experience. The fact remained, none the less, that he thought that all people, whether they be Mexican peons or Russian peasants, whites or Orientals, were capable of being trained in the habits of democracy. "When properly directed," he once declared, "there is no people not fitted for self-government." [13]

These assumptions inevitably had profound implications for Wilson's thought about the development and relationships of nations. His belief in the inherent goodness of man, in progress as the law of organic life and the working out of the divine plan in history, and in democracy as the highest form of government led him straight to the conclusion that democracy must some day be the universal rule of political life. It ultimately led him even further, to the belief that a peaceful world community, governed by a universal public opinion and united for mutual advancement, could exist only when democracy was itself triumphant everywhere. This conviction was

---

[13] Samuel G. Blythe, "Mexico: The Record of a Conversation with President Wilson," *Saturday Evening Post*, CLXXXVI (May 23, 1914), 4.

more than an assumption underlying Wilson's foreign
policy; it was also an imperative force that propelled him
into bold plans for Mexico, the Caribbean region, and,
afterward, the entire world.

The final main assumptions of Wilson's thought about
international relations grew out of his attempt to define
America's role in world affairs within the context of his
general principles and in light of the contribution that the
United States could make. The American people, he believed, had a peculiar role to play, indeed a mission to
execute in history precisely because they were in so many
ways unique among the peoples of the world. They were
unique politically, not because they alone possessed democratic institutions, but because they had succeeded in or-
ganizing diverse sections and a hundred million people
into a federal system such as one day (he at last conceived) must provide a structure for a world organization.
The American people were unique socially, first, because
of their radical affirmation of equality and their historic
repudiation of everything for which the caste- and class-
ridden societies of Europe and Asia stood, and, second,
because they were in fact a new people, the product of
the mixing of all the nationalities of Europe. Finally and
most importantly, they were unique morally and spiritu-
ally. America, Wilson believed, had been born that men
might be free; Americans had done more than any other
people to advance the cause of human welfare; Americans,
above all other peoples, were " custodians of the spirit of
righteousness, of the spirit of equal-handed justice, of the
spirit of hope which believes in the perfectibility of the
law with the perfectibility of human life itself."

Thus America's mission in the world was not to attain
wealth and power, but to fulfill the divine plan by service
to mankind, by leadership in moral purposes, and above

all by advancing peace and world brotherhood. As one scholar has written in summary of Wilson's view:

> [America's] mission was to realize an ideal of liberty, provide a model of democracy, vindicate moral principles, give examples of action and ideals of government and righteousness to an interdependent world, uphold the rights of man, work for humanity and the happiness of men everywhere, lead the thinking of the world, promote peace,—in sum, to serve mankind and progress.[14]

These assumptions and ideals bore so heavily upon the formation of Wilson's foreign policies that we cannot be content with a mere description of them. We must also attempt to see the way in which they equipped or unfitted the President for the needs of practical statesmanship during a critical period.

Only a confirmed cynic would fail to recognize that a large measure of Wilson's strength as a diplomatist and much of his contribution in the field of international relations derived in the first instance from his spiritual resources. To begin with, there were certain practical advantages in idealism. By rejecting narrow nationalism and materialism as bases for foreign policy, and by articulating the noblest traditions of Western culture, Wilson could and did speak as with universal authority, whether in pleading with the Imperial German government to respect human life in using the submarine, in proclaiming a people's war for justice as much to the vanquished as to the victors, or in appealing for a world organization based upon the ideals of peace and co-operation. That is to say, ideals are a dynamic force in cultures that acknowledge their validity, and Wilson was a more effective war leader, a more fearful antagonist of the German mili-

---

[14] Harley Notter, *Origins of the Foreign Policy of Woodrow Wilson*, p. 653.

tary dictators on the ideological battlefield, and a more indomitable fighter for a just peace settlement because he stood for what most men in the Western world (including his opponents) were willing to acknowledge were their own best ideals. Besides, on several occasions, particularly in his relations with Mexico, he was able to escape the consequences of a blundering policy only because he had made his real, that is, his ideal, purposes clear.

We should not measure the significance of Wilson's idealism in practical terms alone. Men violate or more often simply ignore the ideals by which they profess to live; but without ideals to recall lost visions and to give guidance for the present and future, societies degenerate into tyrannies of individuals, classes, or ideologies. It was Wilson's great contribution that while hatreds and passions threatened to wreck Western civilization, he held high the traditions of humanity and the ideal of justice, and by so doing he helped to salvage them for a future generation.

It does not detract from the significance of the foregoing to point out that Wilson's assumptions and principles also impaired to some degree his leadership in the mundane affairs of state. This was true in the first place because his philosophy and thought, even more about foreign than about domestic matters, failed to take sufficient account of what theologians call original sin or what diplomatic specialists call " realities." The qualifying adjective *sufficient* has a key importance here. Wilson was never a fool or a visionary incapable of facing reality; he was keenly intelligent and often shrewd. And yet his faith in the goodness and rationality of men, in the miraculous potentialities of democracy, and in the inevitable triumph of righteousness sometimes caused him to make illusory appraisals of the situations at hand and to devise quixotic or unworkable solutions.

In executing foreign policy generally, Wilson assumed that foreign relations among the great powers consisted of intercourse between civilized gentlemen controlled by an enlightened public opinion and common moral standards, and that decency, good will, and free discussion sufficed to settle all international disputes. This assumption in turn led him to rely mainly upon enlightened instruments of diplomacy—conciliation treaties, the invocation of universal principles in diplomatic correspondence, and displays of friendship—and, conversely, almost to refuse to think in terms of threat or violence. His dependence upon moral suasion in the protracted controversy with Germany over the submarine is one example of his nearly inveterate reliance upon the spirit rather than the sword in foreign relations.

In the second place, Wilson's uncommon concern with the fundamental principles of national and international life sometimes led him to oversimplify the vast complexities of international politics. This deficiency stemmed also from his methods of thinking and arriving at conclusions—methods that were as much intuitive as rational and deductive rather than inductive; it stemmed also from his tendency to invoke analogies between domestic and international politics without taking sufficient account of the enormous differences between the two.

There is a good example of the danger of an almost exclusive reliance upon general principles in the formation of foreign policy in the manner in which Wilson dealt with an important Far Eastern question in 1913, the issue of American participation in the Six-Power Consortium, which had been formed in 1911 to supply capital to the Chinese government. The full records of his discussions about this matter reveal clearly how Wilson's mind worked in making policy. First he set up the general propositions that the European and Japanese governments involved in the Consortium were scheming in the usual imperialistic manner to impair Chinese sovereignty and to gain control over the internal affairs of a democracy struggling to be born. Reasoning deductively, Wilson quickly concluded what the American government should do in these circumstances. Since imperialism and such an attempt to subvert a democracy in its birth were morally wrong, the United States should withdraw from the Consortium and should help the Chinese people in other and more honorable ways.

It was a " moral " decision, based upon reasoning not altogether unsound as far as it went. The trouble was that the Chinese situation in 1913, domestic and external, could not be encompassed by a few moralizations that ignored the unpleasant realities—the fact that Chinese sovereignty was well nigh a fiction, that there was no Chinese " democracy," and that China desperately needed capital to survive. The consequence of Wilson's " moral " decision were soon obvious: The American withdrawal caused the virtual collapse of the Consortium, and the failure of the Western powers to extend financial assistance weakened the Chinese government precisely at the time when the Japanese were beginning their first great drive to control their continental neighbor.[15]

An even more important example of the consequences of oversimplification through too much reliance upon obvious moral principles was Wilson's response to the situation created in Mexico in 1913 when a military usurper, General Victoriano Huerta, overthrew a constitutional government headed by Francisco Madero. To Wilson the issues were as plain as daylight, and he refused on moral grounds to recognize the Huerta government even though it controlled most of Mexico and was constitutional in

[15] For an extended discussion, see the excellent study by Tien-yi Li, *Woodrow Wilson's China Policy, 1913–1917* (New York, 1952).

form. More than this, Wilson went on to devise a new
test of recognition for Mexico, which he later applied to
the Bolshevik regime in Russia. It was a test of constitutional legitimacy, which involved going behind the exterior
to determine whether a government was legitimate, or
politically moral, as well as constitutional in form or *de
facto* in authority.[16] It was " moral " diplomacy, but it
soon involved Wilson and the American government in
far-reaching meddling in the internal affairs of Mexico,
and this in turn led to consequences nearly disastrous for
both countries.[17]

But let us return to my analysis of the way in which
Wilson's assumptions and principles impaired his statesmanship in the field of foreign relations. I have already
mentioned his tendency to take insufficient account of
hard realities and to oversimplify the complexities of
international life. A third point was the unreal quality
of some of his thought and policy that resulted from his
almost romantic faith in the sufficiency of democratic
solutions. This was revealed in his attempts to apply constitutional and democratic criteria to Central America and
the Caribbean states,[18] to the revolutionary upheaval in
Mexico led by Madero's successors, the Constitutionalists,
and finally to the revolutionary situation in Russia between the fall of the czarist government and the triumph
of the Bolsheviks.[19] In all these situations ordinary democratic concepts simply did not apply, yet Wilson insisted

[16] Howard F. Cline, *The United States and Mexico* (Cambridge, Mass.,
1953), p. 142, has an illuminating discussion of this point.

[17] I have told this story at length elsewhere, in *Wilson: The New Freedom,*
pp. 347-416, and in *Woodrow Wilson and the Progressive Era* (New York,
1954), pp. 107-44.

[18] As Samuel Flagg Bemis has pointed out in a telling way in " Woodrow
Wilson and Latin America," MS in possession of the present writer.

[19] George F. Kennan, *Soviet-American Relations, 1917–1920, Russia Leaves
the War* (Princeton, N. J., 1956), particularly pp. 140-48.

upon believing that solutions lay in the establishment of enlightened and responsible governments through free elections.

The fourth and final peril of an excessive concern for ideals and principles in foreign policy was in Wilson's case particularly acute. It was the danger of Pharisaism, which often results from too much introspective concern about the standards of right conduct. It was revealed, among other things, in Wilson's assumption that his motives and purposes were purer than those of the men with whom he happened to be contending. Even though they were actually often well grounded, such convictions left little room for a saving humility and gave Wilson the appearance of the Pharisee who thanked God that he was better than other men.

In the final reckoning, Wilson will be judged not so much by what he thought about foreign policy as by what he did, and I conclude this introductory lecture with a word about his techniques and methods as a diplomatist. They stemmed in an all-pervasive way from his temperament, and we can ease some of the problems that puzzle the biographer if we begin by frankly confronting those aspects of his personality that bore directly upon his practice of leadership. Endowed with an intense nervous and emotional constitution, Wilson was in temperament an extreme activist, never satisfied with mere speculation or willing to apply slow-working remedies, but driven as if by demons to almost frenzied efforts to achieve immediate and ideal solutions.

Was the challenge one of transforming Princeton into a leading institution of higher learning in the United States? Then the task had to be done thoroughly and at once, and no vested social interest or obstreperous individuals could be permitted to stand in the way. As Wilson

put it, all had to be " digested in the processes of the
university." Did the job at hand encompass the reform
of federal economic policies? Then Congress must be
driven and public opinion must be maintained at a high
pitch of excitement in order that all might be finished
during a single congressional session. Were the tasks those
of reconstructing the world order and of propelling the
American people into an international leadership? Then
nothing less than total reconstruction and a total commitment would suffice. This driving force, relentless
energy, and striving for the whole achievement characterized all of Wilson's major efforts in the field of foreign
affairs; they were at once sources of power and of danger.

Two other aspects of personality or temperament had
an equal impact. One was Wilson's egotism, manifested
in his remarkable conviction that he was an instrument
of divine purpose, or his sense of destiny, in his awareness
of his own intellectual superiority over most of his associates, and, above all, in his urge to dominate. The other
was a driving ambition, fired as much by a longing for
personal distinction as by a desire to serve God and mankind. Egotism and ambition combined with a compelling
activism to produce in Woodrow Wilson a leader of extraordinary strength and daring, one who would play not
merely an active but the dominant role in foreign affairs
while he was president.

Mature conviction from scholarly study concerning the
role that the president should play also helped to determine Wilson's methods as a diplomatist. Even during that
period in his scholarly writing when he emphasized congressional government, Wilson recognized the president's
wide latitude in the conduct of affairs abroad. That recognition had grown into a sweeping affirmation of presidential sovereignty by the time that Wilson had reached

maturity in his thought about the American constitutional system.

" One of the greatest of the President's powers," he said in 1907,

> I have not yet spoken of at all: his control, which is very absolute, of the foreign relations of the nation. The initiative in foreign affairs, which the President possesses without any restriction whatever, is virtually the power to control them absolutely. The President cannot conclude a treaty with a foreign power without the consent of the Senate, but he may guide every step of diplomacy, and to guide diplomacy is to determine what treaties must be made, if the faith and prestige of the government are to be maintained. He need disclose no step of negotiation until it is complete, and when in any critical matter it is completed the government is virtually committed. Whatever its disinclination, the Senate may feel itself committed also.[20]

It was a striking characterization of Wilson's own management of foreign affairs a few years after these words were spoken. In the areas that he considered vitally important—Mexico, relations with the European belligerents, wartime relations with the Allied powers, and the writing of a peace settlement—Wilson took absolute personal control. He wrote most of the important notes on his own typewriter, bypassed the State Department by using his own private agents, ignored his secretaries of state by conducting important negotiations behind their backs, and acted like a divine-right monarch in the general conduct of affairs.

Perhaps as good an example of Wilson's personal diplomacy as any I could choose was his handling of the Mexican problem during the period of Huerta's tenure in

[20] *Constitutional Government in the United States,* pp. 77-78.

Mexico City from March, 1913, to August, 1914. Ignoring the men in the State Department who knew anything about the subject, the American Ambasador and the Chargé in the Mexican capital, and the consuls in the field, Wilson proceeded to make a Mexican policy in his own way, as follows: He first sent a journalist whom he trusted, but who knew nothing about Mexican affairs, to Mexico City to investigate. Accepting this reporter's recommendations, Wilson next sent a former Governor of Minnesota, who had neither experience in diplomacy nor any knowledge about Mexico, to present certain proposals for a solution to Huerta. Then, after the Dictator had repudiated the President's right to interfere, Wilson pursued a relentless personal campaign to depose Huerta, one that culminated in armed intervention and Huerta's downfall. Time and again Wilson used the same methods and almost always with the same results: the formation of faulty policy through sheer ignorance, men working at crosspurposes, confusion in the State Department and in the embassies and legations, and the like.

To be sure, there were some extenuating circumstances. Wilson often ignored the professionals in the State Department and the Foreign Service because he genuinely distrusted them, because he thought that they, or many of them, were either aristocrats, the products of exclusive schools and a snobbish society, or else sycophantic imitators of the wealthy classes. "We find," he explained in 1913,

that those who have been occupying the legations and embassies have been habituated to a point of view which is very different, indeed, from the point of view of the present administration. They have had the material interests of individuals in the United States very much more in mind than the moral and public considerations which it seems to us ought to control. They have been so bred in a different school that we have found, in several instances, that it was difficult for them to comprehend our point of view and purpose.[21]

There was also the fact that many of the men through whom Wilson would normally have worked in the conduct of foreign relations *were*, to a varying degree, incompetent, and this because of the necessities of politics and the paucity of Democrats with any experience. Simply and solely because he had to have William J. Bryan's support for domestic policies, Wilson appointed the Great Commoner secretary of state. Because he did not trust Bryan in delicate matters, Wilson turned more and more away from regular channels and leaned increasingly upon unofficial advisers like Colonel Edward M. House.

In the selection of ambassadors for important stations, moreover, Wilson tried desperately to find the best men and to break the custom of using ambassadorships as rewards for party service. Except in a few cases the " best " men would not accept appointment, and Wilson had to yield to pressure and name party hacks to places like Berlin, St. Petersburg, Rome, and Madrid. The classic example was James W. Gerard, a generous contributor to the Democratic treasury and an active Tammany politician, whom Wilson named as ambassador to Germany after vowing that he would never stoop so low. Thus it happened that during a period of extreme tension in German-American relations Wilson had as his spokesman in Berlin a man for whom he had no respect and not a little contempt. The President's opinion of Gerard is rather pungently revealed in the following examples of the comments that he penciled on copies of dispatches from the Ambassador:

[21] Wilson to C. W. Eliot, September 17, 1913, Wilson Papers, Library of Congress.

10 Sept. [1915]

Ordinarily our Ambassador ought to be backed up as
of course, but—this ass? It is hard to take it seriously.
W.

11 Sept. [1915]

Who can fathom this? I wish they would hand this
idiot his passports! W.

As he had not much more confidence in most of his other
ambassadors, it was little wonder that Wilson used them
only as messenger boys.

Thus circumstances that he could not control were
in part responsible for Wilson's extreme individualism in
conducting foreign affairs. Yet they were not entirely
responsible, and the conviction remains that the chief
causes of his exercise of an exclusive personal control were
his urge to dominate, his egotism, and his reasoned jealousy of the presidential power, that is, his belief that it
would be constitutionally dangerous to delegate essential
power for national good or ill to men, even to able men,
not directly responsible to the people.

The essential validity of this conclusion is to some degree revealed in the nature of Wilson's relations with
two men of considerable talents, Robert Lansing and
Walter H. Page. Lansing, who served as counselor of the
State Department from 1914 to 1915 and as secretary of
state from 1915 to 1920, was thoroughly trained in international law and practice, keenly intelligent, and completely loyal to the President. Yet Wilson never really
trusted Lansing's mental processes (once he remarked
that Lansing " was so stupid that he was constantly afraid
he would commit some serious blunder "), never thought
of him as much more than a dignified clerk, and consequently never took full advantage of the resources that
Lansing had to offer.

The reasons for this lack of confidence shed an important light upon the Wilsonian character. To begin with, the two men were fundamentally different in their thought processes: Where Wilson was intuitive and idealistic, Lansing was inductive in reasoning, coldly analytical, and realistic. But the chief cause of Wilson's distrust was Lansing's refusal to give the kind of loyalty that his chief demanded, which was intellectual submission and agreement as well as understanding. Lansing was a little too strong in mind and character thus to subordinate himself, or even to pretend that he did. He survived in office as long as he did only because he became fairly adept in handling the President and only because it was usually inexpedient for Wilson to dismiss him.

Unlike Lansing, Page had no special preparation for his tasks as ambassador to Great Britain, but he had an abundance of natural ability and was soon the master of his functions. So long as he reported what the President wanted to hear, Page was Wilson's intimate friend and best source of opinion abroad, but he soon lost all standing at the White House once he began to offer unwanted advice, to criticize, and to report opinions that disturbed his superior.

Wilson maintained his personal control over foreign policy, finally, by applying the same techniques of leadership of public opinion and of Congress that he used with such spectacular success in domestic struggles. His instruments of public leadership were public papers, statements to the press, and speeches, by means of which he established direct communication with the people and spoke for them in articulating American ideals in foreign policy. Wilson was a spellbinder of immense power during an era when Americans admired oratory above all other political skills, and he was irresistible in leadership so long as he voiced the dominant national sentiments.

In the business of controlling Congress, Wilson's meth-

ods were influenced by his conception of the president as
the unifying force in the federal government. Believing
as he did that the president alone was responsible for the
conduct of foreign relations, he had no thought of a
genuine collaboration with the legislative branch in the
formulation of policies abroad. Believing as he did in
party government and responsibility, Wilson never seriously considered a bipartisan approach to foreign policy.
To be sure, he took careful pains to render periodic ac-
countings to the members of the House and Senate foreign
affairs committees. On several occasions he even asked
Congress to approve policies that he had already decided
to pursue. Yet one has the suspicion that on all these
occasions he was simply observing certain forms in order
to buy congressional support cheaply.

The most revealing examples of Wilson's methods of
dealing with Congress on matters of foreign policy arose,
after all, not during periods of quietude and agreement,
but during times of sharp controversy with the legislative
branch. Wilson's leadership was challenged by a threatened or an actual revolt in Congress on three occasions—
in 1914, during the debate over the repeal of a provision in
the Panama Canal Act of 1912 exempting American coast-
wise shipping from the payment of tolls; in 1916, over the
issue of the right of Americans to travel in safety on
belligerent armed merchant vessels; and in 1919 and 1920,
over ratification of the Treaty of Versailles. To all these
challenges Wilson replied with incredible vigor and bold-
ness. In these important tests Wilson revealed his conviction that in foreign affairs the President should lead
and the Congress should follow.

This ends my account of Wilson's preparation, thought,
and methods as a diplomatist. There are many pitfalls in
such an attempt as I have just made. There are dangers

of overemphasis, of distortion, and of exploring certain aspects of thought and character to such a degree that they seem unique instead of normal. There is the danger of permitting weaknesses in method to assume a larger importance than they deserve in the total estimate. Worse still, there is the danger that inevitably arises when one paints a composite portrait, that of viewing the subject in static form and of forgetting his capacity for growth and his ability to learn by his mistakes. The ordinary risks involved are multiplied when one deals with a person as complex and contradictory as Wilson assuredly was. I only hope that the whole man as diplomatist will reveal himself in all his strength and weakness more fully in the lectures that follow.

CHAPTER II

☙

WILSON *and the problems of neutrality*

FOR WOODROW WILSON and the American people, who had a positive disinclination to play the game of power politics, events on the international stage intruded in an ironic if fateful way from 1914 to 1917. By the spring of 1915 the United States was the only great power not directly involved in the war then raging from western Europe to the Far East. Desiring only to deal fairly with both sides and to avoid military involvement, the President soon found that neutrality, as well as war, has its perplexities and perils.

The way in which Wilson met the challenges to America's peace and security raised by the death grapple between the opposing alliances has never been fully explained, notwithstanding scores of books and articles. Too often, historians, in company with public men, have looked for culprits instead of facts. Too often they have misunderstood the facts even when they found them. Too often they have written as if Wilson and his advisers made policy in a vacuum independent of the interplay of conflicting pressures. If we can see the President's policies of neutrality in the light of his convictions and objectives, the pressures and events (both domestic and foreign) that bore constantly upon him, and the alternatives between which he was often forced to choose—if we can do this, then perhaps we will see that his task in foreign policy at this juncture was not as simple as it has sometimes been described.

Among the most pervasive pressures controlling Wilson's decisions throughout the period 1914–1917 were the attitudes and opinions of the American people concerning the war and America's proper relation to it. Few presidents in American history have been more keenly aware of risks that the leader runs when he ceases to speak for the preponderant majority. " The ear of the leader must ring with the voices of the people. He cannot be of the school of the prophets; he must be of the number of those who studiously serve the slow-paced daily need." Thus Wilson had written in 1890; [1] thus he believed and practiced while formulating his policies toward the belligerents in the First World War.

The dominant American sentiment throughout the period of nonintervention can be summarily characterized by the single adjective " neutral." This is not to say that Americans had no opinions on the merits of the war and the claims of the opposing alliances, or that there were no differences among the popular reactions. It is simply to state the fairly obvious fact that the preponderant majority, whose opinions played a decisive role in shaping Wilson's policies, did not believe that their interests and security were vitally involved in the outcome of the war and desired to avoid participation if that were possible without sacrificing rights that should not be yielded. The prevalence and astounding vitality of neutralism, in spite of the severest provocations and all the efforts of propa-

[1] T. H. Vail Motter (ed.), *Leaders of Men* (Princeton, N. J., 1952), p. 43.

gandists on both sides, formed at once the unifying principle of American politics and the compelling reality with which Wilson had to deal from 1914 to 1917.

On the other hand, it would be a large error to imply that Wilson was a prisoner of the public opinion of the majority, and that his will to adopt sterner policies toward one group of belligerents or the other was paralyzed by the stronger counterforce of neutralism. Actually, the evidence points overwhelmingly to the conclusion that Wilson personally shared the opinions of the majority, in brief, that he was substantially neutral in attitude, and that his policies were controlled as much by his own convictions as by the obvious wishes of the people.

Never once throughout the period of American neutrality did Wilson explain by word of mouth or set down in writing his personal views on the causes and merits of the war. However, this does not mean that one is entirely helpless in trying to reconstruct his methods of thinking and the character of his thought about this subject. There is some direct and considerably more circumstantial evidence to indicate that he set up certain general principles and assumptions at the outset and reasoned deductively from them to form his conclusions.

One of these assumptions was Wilson's belief that the causes of the war were enormously complex and obscure. The conflict, he believed, had its origins in the divisive nationalisms of the Austro-Hungarian Empire, in Russia's drive for free access to the Mediterranean, in France's longing for the recovery of Alsace-Lorraine, in Germany's challenge to Britain's naval and commercial supremacy, in the system of rival alliances that had grown up following the Franco-Prussian War, and in the general imperialistic rivalries of the late nineteenth and early twentieth centuries. At no time in correspondence or conversation did he ever say, " These are the important root causes of the war." Nevertheless, he revealed conclusively that he thought that they were when he first singled them out as prime causes of international conflict that would have to be removed if the world were ever to achieve a lasting peace.

It followed in Wilson's mind, then, that all the belligerents shared to some degree in the responsibility for the war and that one could not ascribe all blame to one side or the other. Nor could one use simple explanations in talking about conflicting war objectives. It was clear to Wilson that all the belligerents sincerely believed that they were fighting for their existence, but that all of them desired a smashing victory in order to enhance their power, win new territory, and impose crushing indemnities upon their enemies. Because this was true, Wilson reasoned, the best kind of settlement would be a stalemate in which neither alliance would have the power to impose terms upon the other.

In his fundamental thinking about war in general, moreover, Wilson shared in a remarkable way the assumptions of the majority of Americans. Like most of his fellow-citizens, he abhorred the very thought of using violence to achieve national objectives; indeed, he was reluctant to use even the threat of force in diplomacy. Like the Socialists, independent radicals, and a large majority of southern and western farmers, he suspected that the financiers and industrialists favored preparedness and a strong foreign policy in order to increase profits and provoke a war that would end the reform movement at home. Like the majority of Americans, he was willing to think of fighting only as a last resort and then only as a means of defending rights that no civilized nation could yield.

Fortified by these convictions, Wilson struggled hard and on the whole successfully to be impartial in thought as well as in deed, as he had asked the American people at the outbreak of the war to do. In fact, he succeeded in this impossible undertaking far better than most of his contemporaries and his historical critics. His method was to rely upon the general assumptions that he was sure were sound and then virtually to seal himself off from the passionate arguments and indictments of partisans of either alliance, by simply refusing to listen to them. " I recall," Secretary Lansing afterward wrote, for example, " that . . . his attitude toward evidence of German atrocities in Belgium and toward accounts of the horrors of submarine warfare . . . [was that] he would not read of them and showed anger if the details were called to his attention." [2]

This does not mean that Wilson was able completely to subordinate emotional reactions and personal feelings. Like the majority of Americans, he was to a degree pro-British; on two, perhaps three, occasions during the two and a half years of American neutrality he avowed to close friends his personal sympathy for the Allied cause. But it would be a difficult task to prove that Wilson's pro-British sympathies were ever controlling or indeed even very strong. At no time did he act like a man willing to take measures merely to help his supposed friends. On the contrary, all his policies were aimed either at averting American participation on Britain's side or at ending the war on terms that would have denied the spoils of victory to Britain and her allies. If this is too big an assertion to be taken on faith, then perhaps the reasons for making it will become apparent as we see the way in which Wilson executed policies toward the two leading antagonists.

All authorities, whether friendly or hostile to Wilson, would agree that the acid tests of his neutrality were

[2] The Diary of Robert Lansing, November 20, 1921, MS in the Library of Congress.

the policies that he worked out and applied vis-à-vis the British from 1914 to 1917. He has been most condemned by that group of historians highly censorious of his policies, generally known as revisionists, on this score—for becoming the captive of pro-Allied influences within his administration, for condoning such sweeping British control of neutral commerce that the Germans were forced to resort to drastic countermeasures, for permitting American prosperity to become dependent upon loans and exports to the Allies, in short, for permitting a situation to develop that made it inevitable that the United States would go to war if the success of Allied arms was ever seriously threatened.

Like most fallacious arguments, this one contains a certain element of plausibility. Wilson did condone a far-reaching British maritime system. American neutrality did work greatly to the benefit of the Allies. The error arises in saying that these things occurred because Wilson and his advisers necessarily wanted them to occur.

Perhaps the best way to gain a clear understanding of why Anglo-American relations developed as they did from 1914 to 1917 is to see how the policies that decisively shaped those relations emerged in several stages in response to certain pressures, events, and forces. The first stage, lasting from August, 1914, to about August, 1915, was in many ways the most critical, because the basic American response to the war and to the British maritime system was formulated then. That response was governed in the first instance by two domestic realities: the overwhelming, virtually unanimous, American desire to be neutral, and the pressures in the United States for a large measure of free trade with Britain's enemies.

In view of the prevailing American sentiment at the outbreak of the war, a policy of strict official neutrality was the only possible course for the United States govern-

ment. This fact prompted the President's official procla-
mations of neutrality, supplemented by his appeal to the
American people for impartiality in thought; the subsequent working out by the State Department of the elaborate technical rules to preserve American neutrality;
and the establishment of a Joint State and Navy Neutrality Board to advise the various departments upon the
correct interpretation of international law.

One cannot read the records revealing how these policies
were formulated without being convinced that their
authors were high-minded in their determination to be
fair to both sides. Indeed, Wilson and the man who chiefly
influenced him in the formulation of the rules of neutrality,
Secretary of State Bryan, were so intent upon being fair
to the Germans that they adopted policies during the first
months of the war that were highly disadvantageous to
the British, if not unneutral. One was to prevent the sale
of submarine parts, and hence parts for any naval craft,
by a private American firm to the British government,
on the ground that such a sale would be " contrary to . . .
strict neutrality." Wilson persisted in supporting Bryan
in this matter, in spite of advice from Counselor Lansing
and the Joint Neutrality Board to the effect that their
position was contrary to international law.

Infinitely more damaging to the Allies was the administration's second effort to lean over backward in being
" strictly " neutral—the ban of loans by American bankers
to the belligerent governments that the President permitted Bryan to impose in August, 1914. From a technical
viewpoint, the ban was not unneutral, but it was highly
prejudicial to the Allies because its effect was potentially
to deny them their otherwise legal right to purchase supplies in the American market. These two incidents are
not to be understood as revealing any anti-British bias
on the part of Wilson and Bryan, although British officials

at the time were convinced that they did. I mention them only to show what an important role the administration's desire to be impartial played in the formation of policies vis-à-vis the British during the early period of American neutrality.

The other pressure shaping American policies at this time was the force of combined demands at home for the virtually free transit of American ships and goods to the European neutrals and the belligerent Central Powers. So powerful were these demands, especially from cotton growers and exporters and their spokesmen in Congress, that Wilson personally sponsored two measures highly disadvantageous to the British and unneutral in fact as well as in spirit. One was a change in the ship registry law, put into effect by an act approved August 18, 1914, which made it easy for German or other foreign shipping firms to take out American registry for their vessels. The other was a plan to establish a federal corporation to purchase German ships in American ports and to use them to carry supplies to the belligerents, particularly to Germany. Wilson applied heavy pressure to obtain congressional approval of this, the so-called ship-purchase bill, during the short term from December, 1914, to March, 1915; he failed only because of a stout senatorial filibuster.

In negotiations with the British government during the early months of the war, Wilson fought hard in response to domestic pressures to keep the channels of international commerce open to American ships and goods. He did not go as far in defense of neutral rights as some of his predecessors, but he did suggest a code so sweeping that an enforcement of it would have meant almost total destruction of the British system of maritime controls. Specifically, the President first proposed on August 6, 1914, that the belligerents adopt the rules of naval warfare laid down in the Declaration of London of 1909, a convention never ratified by Great Britain or the United States, which permitted the free transit of all goods except those obviously contraband. When the British rejected this suggestion, the President came back on October 16, proposing a compromise that would have still seriously impaired the effectiveness of British sea power. When this effort also failed, Wilson then announced that his government would assert and defend all its rights under international law and treaties.

I have described these policies and proposals because they so clearly reveal Wilson's neutral intentions and what he would have done in matters of trade had he been able to make the rules himself. But he obviously could not follow his personal preferences alone or respond only to domestic pressures. In seeking to assert and defend American neutral rights he ran head-on into a reality as important as the reality of the pressures at home. It was the British determination to use sea power to prevent American ships and goods from going to the sustenance of the German economy and military forces.

British assumption of a nearly absolute control of the seas washing western Europe began with relatively mild measures in August, 1914, and culminated in the suppression of virtually all commerce to the Central Powers in March, 1915. For the British, this was not a question of adhering to the laws of blockade or of violating them, or of doing things merely to be nice to American friends. It was a question of achieving their supreme objective, to deprive their enemies of vital raw materials and goods, without risking the alienation of the United States. The controlling fact for the British was the necessity of preserving American friendship, in order to assure the uninterrupted rhythm of the North Atlantic trade. As the British Foreign Secretary at the time frankly put it:

Blockade of Germany was essential to the victory of the Allies, but the ill-will of the United States meant their certain defeat. . . . It was better therefore to carry on the war without blockade, if need be, than to incur a break with the United States about contraband and thereby deprive the Allies of the resources necessary to carry on the war at all or with any chance of success. The object of diplomacy, therefore, was to secure the maximum of blockade that could be enforced without a rupture with the United States.[3]

The crucial question all along, therefore, was whether the United States, the only neutral power strong enough successfully to challenge the British measures, would acquiesce or resist to the point of threatening or using force. The American response during the formative period of neutrality was, in brief, to accept the British system and to limit action against it to a vigorous assertion of American legal rights for future adjudication. All this is too well known to require any further exposition. What is not so well understood are the reasons why Wilson and his advisers acquiesced in a solution that denied the objectives that they and a large segment of the American public demanded. These reasons may be briefly summarized, as follows:

First, the British maritime system, in spite of American allegations to the contrary, enjoyed the advantage of being legitimate and usually legal, or nearly so, by traditional criteria. It was legitimate rather than fraudulent, and legal rather than capricious or terroristic, in its major aspects because the British did in fact hold undisputed sea supremacy and were therefore able to execute their controls in an orderly fashion. In asserting their own rights, the Americans could not well deny the advantages that ac-

---

[3] Viscount Grey of Fallodon, *Twenty-Five Years, 1892–1916* (2 vols.; New York, 1925), II, 107.

crued to the British by virtue of their sea power. The British, for example, had an undoubted right to establish a blockade of the Central Powers, and the American attempt to persuade the London government to use techniques effective only in the days of the sailing ship did not have much cogency in the twentieth century.

Second, much of the success of the British in establishing their control depended upon the way in which they went about it. Had they instituted their total blockade at the outset of the war, the American reaction would undoubtedly have been violent. Instead, the British applied their controls gradually, with a careful eye upon American opinion, using the opportunities provided by recurrent crises in German-American relations to institute their severest measures.

Third, the British were careful never to offend so many American interests at one time that retaliation would have been inevitable, or any single interest powerful enough by itself to compel retaliation. There was the case of cotton, which the officials in London were determined to prevent from going to Germany because it was an ingredient of gunpowder. Not until a year after the war began did they put cotton on the list of absolute contraband; even then they went to the extraordinary length of underwriting the entire American cotton market in order to avert an irresistible southern pressure in Congress for retaliation.[4] In addition, although they were ruthless in enforcing their blockade, the British took careful pains to avoid any serious injury to American property interests. They confiscated only the most obvious contraband; in all doubtful cases they paid full value for cargoes or ships

[4] For a full discussion, see my " The Cotton Crisis, the South, and Anglo-American Diplomacy, 1914–1915," in J. C. Sitterson (ed.), *Studies in Southern History in Memory of Albert Ray Newsome, 1894–1951* (Chapel Hill, N. C., 1957), pp. 122-38.

seized. Their objective was to control, not to destroy, American commerce.

Fourth, there was great significance in the language and symbolism that the British Foreign Office used in defending the measures of the Admiralty and Ministry of Blockade. By justifying their maritime system in terms of international law and the right of retaliation, and (at least before the summer of 1916) by making an honest effort to meet American objections half way when possible, the British made it almost inevitable that the Washington authorities would have to reply in the same language, thus giving a purely *legal* character to the issues involved and for the most part avoiding raising the issues of sovereignty and inherent national rights. The significance of this achievement can be seen in the conviction of Wilson and the majority of Americans that the Anglo-American disputes did involve only property rights, which should be vindicated only by an appeal to much-controverted international law. Moreover, by appealing to the American government and people in the name of friendship and by always professing their devotion to the cause of humanity, the British succeeded in evoking strong feelings of sympathy and understanding on the other side of the water.

Finally, the British were able partially to justify their own blockade measures as legitimate adaptations to a changing technology by pointing to precedents established by the Washington government itself during the American Civil War. To be sure, the British drew some incorrect analogies (as Lansing pointed out) between American and British practice; even so, their main contention—that the American government had also stretched the rules of blockade to allow for technological changes—was essentially correct.

Wilson's refusal to challenge the British maritime system, in short, to break the British blockade, was almost inevitable in view of the facts we have just reviewed, *if the President's objective was simply to maintain as best he could the neutral position of the United States.* An absolute neutrality was in any event impossible because of the total character of the war and America's importance in the world economy. It often happened that any action by the United States inevitably conferred a benefit on one side and thereby injured the other, at least indirectly. In these circumstances, neutrality often consisted of doing the things that would give the least unwarranted or undeserved advantages.

By this standard, it would have been more unneutral than neutral for Wilson to have broken the British maritime system by enforcing highly doubtful technical rights under international law. Judged by practical standards rather than by the often conflicting criteria of neutrality, Wilson's acceptance of the British system seems realistic and wise—indeed, the only choice that he could have made in the circumstances. This is true because the results of destroying the British blockade would have been the wrecking of American friendship with the two great European democracies and the probable victory of the Central Powers, without a single compensating gain for the interests and security of the United States. Only the sure achievement of some great political objective like a secure peace settlement, certainly not the winning of a commercial advantage or the defense of doubtful neutral rights, would have justified Wilson in undertaking a determined challenge to British sea power.

The second stage in Anglo-American relations, lasting from the summer of 1915 to the late spring of 1916, saw the development of the natural economic consequence of the American adjustment to tightening British control of the seas. That consequence was the burgeoning of an enormous war trade between the United States and the Allies. The United States became the storehouse and armory of the Allies neither because there was any conspiracy on the part of certain pro-Allied leaders in Washington to make American prosperity dependent upon an Allied victory, nor because American businessmen and bankers were willing to incur the risks of war in order to increase their profits. The United States became the storehouse of the Allies for the simple reason that Great Britain and not Germany controlled the seas.

The war trade itself was entirely neutral. Indeed, any action by the United States government to impede it, unless undertaken for overriding political motives, would have been grossly prejudicial and unneutral. If it had been permitted to develop in a normal way, this commerce would have raised no important problems in the relations of the United States with the Allies. A problem of the first magnitude did arise, however, because the President, in the summer of 1914, had permitted Secretary Bryan to enforce his own private moral views by imposing a ban on loans by American bankers to the belligerents.

There was no difficulty so long as the British and French governments could find gold and dollars to settle their adverse trade balances. By the summer of 1915, however, Allied gold and dollar resources were near the point of exhaustion; and American insistence upon a continuation of cash payments could result only in gravely damaging the Allied economies and ending the North Atlantic trade altogether. Credit could be found only in the United States, but credit meant floating loans, and loans to the belligerents were as much a political as an economic question because of the existence of Bryan's ban.

It is well known that the State Department under Bryan's direction substantially relaxed its credit embargo during the spring of 1915 and that Wilson and Bryan's successor, Lansing, lifted the ban altogether a few months later, at a time when the credit needs of the Allied governments were demonstrably acute. Even though the full facts bearing upon this matter have been available to scholars for more than twenty years, the reasons for the administration's reversal are still not properly understood.

Bryan's ban could not survive the development of the war trade on a large scale because, in the first place, it (like the Embargo of 1808) was potentially nearly as disastrous to the United States as to the Allies. American material well-being was in large measure dependent upon foreign trade, and particularly upon trade with the Allied world. Such trade was possible during wartime only if American businessmen were willing to do for the Allies what they always did for solvent customers in temporary straits, namely, sell them goods on credit.

The most important reason that Bryan's embargo could not survive, however, was that it was an essentially unneutral policy that impeded the growth of the chief economic consequence of American neutrality, the legitimate war trade. The credit embargo and the war trade could not both survive. The former gave way because Wilson finally realized that it would be as unneutral to interfere with the extension of credit as it would be to stop the flow of goods. Bryan's ban was in a sense, therefore, a casualty chiefly of American neutrality.

The historian can talk himself blue in the face without really convincing his listeners that these simple facts are true. He can point out that Britain's existence depended upon her ability to use sea power to keep the channels of trade and credit open, just as Germany's existence depended upon the use of superior land power. He can demonstrate that the sale of goods and the extension of credit to belligerents by private parties were neutral in theory, tradition, and practice. He can show that the

effect of unwarranted interference with such intercourse
would have been seriously to penalize sea power to the
advantage of land power. But a historian arguing this
way makes little impression upon an American audience,
because the issue is still too supercharged with emotional-
ism and is still resolved within a framework of economic
determinism, of hostility to the business and financial
classes, and of moralistic pacifism.

The second stage in Anglo-American relations also wit-
nessed the apparent convergence of the diplomatic policies
of the two countries on the high level. During the summer
and autumn of 1915 Colonel Edward M. House, Wilson's
confidant and principal adviser on foreign policy, conceived a plan by which the American and British leaders
would join hands to press for an end to the war through
Wilson's mediation. The British Foreign Secretary, Sir
Edward Grey, replied that his government would co-
operate only if the Washington administration were willing to go beyond simple mediation and would agree to
join a postwar international organization established for
the purpose of effecting disarmament, maintaining freedom of the seas, and preserving peace. Wilson hopefully
consented, and House went to Berlin, Paris, and London
in January, 1916, to lay the diplomatic basis of mediation.

In London, House worked out in documentary form
with Grey and the other members of the British Cabinet
the specific terms of Anglo-American co-operation. Initialed by House and Grey on February 22, 1916, and known
as the House-Grey Memorandum or Agreement, this document declared that President Wilson was ready, upon
hearing from England and France that the time was ripe,
to propose that a conference be called to end the war.
Should the Allies accept and Germany refuse the invita-
tion, the United States would " probably " enter the war

against Germany. Should the conference meet and Germany refuse to accept a reasonable settlement, then the United States would also " probably " enter the war on the Allied side.

To the so-called revisionists the conclusion of the House-Grey Agreement is irrefutable proof that Wilson had abandoned neutrality and meant to take the country into war at the first opportunity. To remove all doubt that this was true, they point to what happened during the weeks immediately following the initialing of the agreement.

While House had been carrying his negotiations in London to a succesful conclusion, Wilson and Lansing had undertaken to avert the possibility of conflict with Germany over the issue of submarine attacks against armed merchantmen by proposing that the Allies disarm their merchant ships and that U-boats follow the old rules of cruiser warfare in attacking them. Using the President's suggestion as a pretext, the German authorities announced on February 10, 1916, that submarines would attack *armed* enemy merchantmen without warning after February 29. Then without warning Wilson and Lansing reversed themselves and announced that the American government would insist upon the right of Americans to travel on ships defensively armed and would hold the German government to strict account for the loss of any American lives on armed merchantmen. Adhering doggedly to this position in the face of a threatened rebellion in Congress, the President proceeded to use the opportunity afforded by the torpedoing without warning of the French Channel packet *Sussex* by a German submarine, " in contravention of earlier pledges," to threaten a break in diplomatic relations with Germany and to force the Imperial government to make sweeping concessions in its conduct of submarine warfare.

To the revisionist critics, the case is so clear that it
needs no further proof. The House-Grey Agreement, they
say, was conceived and concluded for the purpose of promoting early American intervention. Wilson at once
sought to accomplish this goal by taking a position on
armed merchant ships that was bound to provoke a crisis
with Germany, and by pressing the German government
so hard during the *Sussex* controversy that a break in
relations would probably ensue. The plan failed, the revisionists explain, only because the violent opposition in
Congress convinced the President that the lawmakers
would never approve a declaration of war to uphold the
right of Americans to travel on belligerent armed merchant ships, and only because the German authorities
proved to be more conciliatory than Wilson had expected.

The revisionists are correct in asserting that the conclusion of the House-Grey Agreement marked the beginning of a new and epochal phase in Wilson's policies
toward the belligerents. Otherwise they have missed the
entire meaning of the affair, for the House-Grey Agreement was in Wilson's purpose *not an instrument of intervention, but a means of averting American involvement.*
The truth of this important generalization will perhaps become evident when we recall the realities of the American
diplomatic situation during late 1915 and early 1916, and
when we understand Wilson's motives and intentions in
devising a solution.

The overshadowing reality confronting the makers of
American foreign policy at this time was the grave possibility of war with Germany over the submarine issue. It
caused Wilson and Lansing, for example, to abandon
ambitious plans for further intervention in Mexico. It
speeded the American acquiescence in the British maritime
system. Most important, it prompted the President and

his advisers to search for ways to avert the rupture that might draw the United States into the maelstrom.

One way out of the predicament was to come to a full understanding with the German government over the issues involved in the submarine controversy. This is what Lansing attempted to do and almost succeeded in accomplishing during his negotiations over the *Lusitania* affair. Another way out and a surer means of averting the peril of American involvement in the future was to bring the war itself to an end through Wilson's mediation. It seemed at the time that the best hope of peace lay in Anglo-American co-operation for a peace of compromise, specifically in the kind of co-operation detailed in the House-Grey Agreement.

Thus Wilson approved this plan of mediation, but with a full realization that certain obligations and risks were involved. There was the necessity of giving positive assurances to the Allies, for they would have been at a fatal disadvantage in a peace conference without American support, in view of the strategic advantages that the Germans then enjoyed on the Continent of Europe. There was, moreover, the risk of war if the Germans refused to approve an armistice or proved to be unreasonable at a peace conference after agreeing to end the fighting. However, Wilson gave the necessary assurances in the belief that the risk of war involved was insignificant as compared to the greater danger of hostilities with Germany if he could not somehow bring the war to an end. This, then, was his dominant motive in sending House to Europe in January, 1916, and in approving the House-Grey Agreement at the cost of Lansing's proposed compromise for submarine warfare.

In the final analysis, our judgment of Wilson's mediation plans must depend upon the kind of settlement that he had in mind and for which he was willing to run the risk of war in order to achieve peace. It is clear that Wilson envisaged a " reasonable " settlement based upon recognition that the war was a stalemate and upon a return for the most part of the *status quo ante bellum*. It meant, Wilson also hoped, the kind of settlement in which all the belligerents would forego annexations and indemnities, put aside past differences, and join hands with the United States to create a new international order. In his final discussions with the British Cabinet, Colonel House made it clear that this, and this only, was the kind of settlement that Wilson was prepared to use the House-Grey Agreement to achieve. In other words, as House told the British leaders, the President would " throw the weight of the United States on the side of those wanting a just settlement—a settlement which would make another such war impossible." [5]

Granted that Wilson's purpose was a genuinely neutral mediation, we can almost hear the critics say, how can one explain his seemingly provocative stand during the crises over armed merchantmen and the *Sussex*? Was he not making such a bold assertion of American rights in the hope that the German government would deny them and thereby give him an excuse for going to Congress for a declaration of war?

The answer, again, is that Wilson was trying desperately to prepare the way for peace and not for war. He and Lansing had proposed the disarming of merchant ships in the hope that this would facilitate a definitive understanding with Germany. But, as House and Page pointed out in urgent telegrams from London, such a proposal was unneutral in spirit and if implemented might mean the destruction of the British merchant marine; and Wilson's insistence upon it would assuredly disqualify him as a

[5] The Diary of Edward M. House, February 14, 1916, MS in the Yale University Library.

mediator acceptable to the Allies. Wilson suddenly reversed himself on the armed ship issue, therefore, primarily in order to restore his neutral standing. Then, following the conclusion of the House-Grey Agreement, the President pressed the Germans for guarantees of good behavior in the conduct of their submarine operations. But he did this with agonizing reluctance because of the risk of war involved and only in order to create a situation in which he might begin to move for peace.

All of Wilson's actions during the third and final stage in American neutrality, lasting from early May, 1916, to early February, 1917, confirm these conclusions. I will discuss his efforts to avert American involvement and his plans for peace in the next lecture. Let us now see how he had meanwhile worked out his response to the continuing challenge of the submarine, and why.

So long as the British controlled the seas and the Germans commanded the strategic territories and resources of Europe, the American task of neutrality was the relatively easy one of accepting a *de facto* situation and of pursuing the most impartial policies possible within this framework of power. Thus Wilson permitted the German invasion of Belgium to pass without protest, even though some Americans contended that he was morally obliged to denounce such a gross violation of international law; thus he accepted the British maritime system. In this situation of actual stalemate, there was little likelihood of an Anglo-American rupture and no possibility of a German-American conflict, because there were no points of friction between the two governments. But the German decision to attempt to break the stalemate by using an untried weapon, the submarine, created a situation of great peril for the United States because it raised the issue of fundamental national rights and made it exceedingly difficult for the President to continue to steer a neutral course. Before we see how he struggled to find some adjustment to this new situation, let us consider for a moment some of the underlying factors that helped to govern German submarine policy and Wilson's response.

First, German decisions regarding the use of the submarine were determined almost exclusively by internal and objective considerations—the number of submarines on hand and their calculated effectiveness, the military situation in Europe and how it might be affected by American intervention, and the like—and in no essential way by American policies vis-à-vis the British, or by the rules of international law for cruiser warfare. Many historians have assumed that stern American resistance to the British maritime system, resulting in opening the channels of trade in noncontraband materials to the Central Powers, would have rendered the so-called submarine blockade unnecessary. This conclusion assumes that the Germans used the submarine only to force the British to abandon their own blockade. Actually, the chief and in the final showdown the only reason the Germans used the submarine was to cut Britain off from her indispensable sources of supply and thereby to win the war. To put the proposition in its strongest form, the Germans would have used the submarine to knock England out of the war when they had enough U-boats to accomplish this goal, even if the British had long since given up their maritime system altogether. That is to say, calculations of sheer military advantage or disadvantage and not American or even British maritime policies dictated the way in which the Germans would prosecute their underseas campaign.

Second, the submarine was in 1915 a new weapon of naval warfare. This was an important fact, for it meant that there was no special international law to govern its use when the rights of neutrals were involved. The only laws that could be applied were the rules of cruiser warfare, which required attacking warships to warn merchant ships before sinking them and to make provision for the safety of passengers and crew. The trouble was that the submarine was not a cruiser, but a frail craft that had to rely upon deception and quick striking power for safety and effectiveness. If its use had been an issue only between the belligerents, then international law would not have been much involved. But international law was directly involved, because its provisions defined not only the rights of neutrals, but their obligations to the belligerent powers as well. Having chosen a course of neutrality under international law, Wilson had to work within accepted rules in formulating his response to the submarine challenge insofar as American rights were concerned. The Allies, understandably, would not consent to modifications to permit enemy submarines to operate at their peak deadly efficiency; their refusal made it difficult for Wilson to insist upon changing the rules without seeming to be unneutral in spirit and without in fact conferring enormous advantages upon the Germans.

Third, all questions of international law aside, a great power like the United States could not view the submarine blockade as a legitimate weapon, one that should be considered and perhaps accepted on grounds of expediency or necessity. This was true because at the time of its inauguration in February, 1915, the submarine blockade was actually a sham, since the Germans were then able to keep at most only seven U-boats at one time in all the waters surrounding the British Isles. The Germans, in fact, inaugurated the " blockade " with four submarines in service in the area. A year later, at the time of the *Sussex* crisis, the German Admiralty could send only eleven or twelve submarines into western waters at one time. Knowledge of these facts decisively influenced the way in which Wilson and his advisers viewed the so-called blockade and formulated policies regarding it, for it was one of the oldest and most generally recognized rules of international law that a blockade must be effective in order to be legal.

Fourth, unlike the Anglo-American disputes over trading rights, which involved only property interests, the German submarine campaign as it was often prosecuted raised an issue which no great power should ever evade or arbitrate—the safety and welfare of its people in pursuits and areas where they have a right to be. It is almost inconceivable that Wilson and the American people could have thought of going to war with the British over issues of search and seizure or of blockade. It is also inconceivable that they would not have been willing to think in terms of war with a government that permitted, indeed, instructed, its naval commanders to slaughter Americans indiscriminately upon the high seas.

It would, however, be a mistake of almost fatal magnitude to conclude, as so many writers have done, that Wilson's response to the submarine challenge was a simple and automatic reaction governed entirely by these factors. Although they played an important role, Wilson actually formed and executed, not a single consistent submarine policy, but a series of policies in response to changing issues and circumstances and in response to his own larger diplomatic objectives.

His first policy was formed in answer to the original German proclamation of submarine warfare. Avoiding the more difficult issue raised, the one involving the right of Americans to travel in safety on belligerent ships, Wilson replied by simply but strongly affirming the right of American vessels to use the seas subject to limitations permitted by international law, and by warning that the United States would hold Germany to a " strict accountability " (Counselor Lansing's words) for lives and property lost as a consequence of illegal submarine attacks against *American neutral* shipping. It was the only position that the President could have taken without abandoning the pretense of neutrality and national dignity, and the Germans soon retreated and gave such sweeping guarantees regarding American ships that this issue was never again a point of conflict between the two governments before 1917.

There still remained the necessity of devising a policy to deal with the more controversial issue of the right of American citizens to travel and work on *belligerent* merchant ships under conditions of safety specified by international law. When a German submarine sank the British liner *Falaba* without warning in March, 1915, killing an American citizen, Wilson's advisers in the State Department squared off in a momentous debate over the formulation of a proper response. One group, headed by Secretray Bryan, argued that American interests were not sufficiently involved to warrant a stern protest against submarine attacks on Allied ships, even when Americans were traveling on them, and that the spirit of neutrality demanded that the United States condone German violations of international law as it had done with British violations. The other group, headed by Counselor Lansing, replied that the attack on the *Falaba* had been such a flagrant infraction of international law that the United States must protest uncompromisingly in order to defend its neutrality and honor.

The records reveal that Wilson would have preferred to avoid any involvement while the two giant belligerents fought it out on the seas. In legal theory he agreed with Lansing, but he was so strongly moved by Bryan's pleading that he had apparently decided by the end of the debate over a *Falaba* note to make no protest at all. This is the course that he would probably have followed in the future if the Germans, by confining their underseas campaign to attacks against Allied cargo ships and by showing a desire to avoid the loss of American life, had made it possible for him to find a means of adjusting to the new situation.

A policy of noninvolvement, however, became impossible when a German U-boat sank the British passenger liner *Lusitania* without warning on May 7, 1915, with the loss of almost 1,200 civilians, including 128 Americans, men, women, and children. Wilson had to make some positive response now, so atrocious was the deed in the eyes of the American people, so flagrant was the violation of elemental national rights, so unneutral and degrading would be an acceptance of the terror campaign against the North Atlantic passenger liners.

The strategic facts of the situation—the German inability to maintain any effective blockade of the British Isles and the consequent serious dangers to Germany from a break with the United States—would have justified the President in peremptorily demanding prompt disavowal and guarantees. Wilson's response, however, reflected his own desire and that of the majority of Americans to preserve neutrality and to avoid taking any position short of yielding essential rights that might lead to hostilities with Germany. Thus all during the summer of 1915 Wilson pounded out notes on his typewriter, for the sole purpose of persuading the German government to disavow the sinking of the *Lusitania* and to abandon its campaign against unarmed passenger vessels. Threatening to break relations after a U-boat sank the liner *Arabic* on August 19, 1915, Wilson finally won the promise that he demanded.

By the end of the summer of 1915 the President had thus worked through two stages of policy and had won immunity from ruthless submarine attacks on American neutral ships and unarmed belligerent passenger liners.

Up to this time, at any rate, Wilson had been patient, conciliatory, and firm only in his demand that the Germans give up measures that had already taken American lives and threatened untold others.

The third stage in the formulation of Wilson's policies toward the submarine, lasting from the early autumn of 1915 through the *Sussex* crisis in the spring of 1916, saw the President attempting to reach a definitive understanding with the Berlin authorities over all phases of submarine warfare against merchant shipping. The issue was daily becoming more difficult to solve by the application of traditional law, because the Allies since March, 1915, had been arming some passenger and cargo ships and ordering them to attack submarines that showed " hostile intent." But Wilson and Lansing persisted in trying to find a solution in spite of the obstacles because they (or Wilson, at any rate) and the majority of Americans still earnestly desired to avoid conflict over merely technical issues.

By patient negotiation Lansing finally won something resembling a German apology for the loss of American lives on the *Lusitania* and an implicit reaffirmation of the *Arabic* pledge. In order to hasten this German concession and to avert even the possibility of future contention, Lansing proposed his *modus vivendi* of January 18, 1916 (already mentioned), designed to provide a new code to govern the German underseas campaign against maritime commerce. This was the proposal that the Allies disarm their merchant ships and that the German submarines observe the rules of cruiser warfare in attacking them.

Adoption of the proposal by the opposing belligerents, or by the United States and Germany alone, would have achieved Wilson's objective of a comprehensive settlement of the submarine issue. And yet, for reasons that we have already seen, Wilson jettisoned the *modus vivendi* in order to save the House-Grey Agreement. Soon afterward,

during the *Sussex* controversy (as we have also seen), he
launched a new campaign to force the German government to conduct submarine operations against all merchant ships, armed and unarmed, within the rules of
cruiser warfare.

Wilson's rejection of the opportunity to come to a
seemingly definitive understanding with Germany seems
altogether logical and wise when we remember his objectives and the circumstances in which he made these
decisions during the third stage in German-American relations. Wilson's supreme objective now was peace through
his own mediation. Mediation seemed possible at this
time only through the co-operation of the British government. But the British would co-operate only if they believed that the President was genuinely neutral, and
certainly not if he insisted upon a code of submarine
warfare that minimized the risks to Americans at the
expense of British sea power to the advantage of an essentially illegitimate weapon.

Mediation was a noble objective with such great bene-
fits to the United States that it justified taking a few
risks to achieve. But Wilson could have followed no other
course than the one he followed during the crises over
armed merchantmen and the *Sussex*, even if his objective
had been merely to maintain American neutrality. In
the circumstances prevailing in the late winter of 1916,
Wilson had to choose between continuing to accept the
British maritime system, mooted by American Civil War
precedents, or acquiescing in the challenge to that system,
the German submarine blockade. The first was legitimate
because it was based upon *de facto* power as well as legal
precedent; the second was not legitimate because it was
still a paper blockade without any power of effective enforcement. By insisting upon adherence to traditional
rules insofar as the rights of Americans were concerned,

Wilson was not at this time depriving the Germans of a weapon essential for their survival or one the free use of which would bring them victory at this time. This, essentially, was the reason that they yielded (for the time being) to Wilson's demands in the *Sussex* crisis. By insisting upon the adoption of Lansing's *modus vivendi,* on the other hand, Wilson in effect would have changed the traditional rules and aimed a heavy blow at the British maritime system, and only for the illusory purpose of averting the possibility of a conflict with Germany.

The final test of any foreign policy is whether it serves the national interest. If it was to the interest of the United States to avoid participation in the war at any cost, regardless of its outcome, and if implementing the *modus vivendi* would have averted all possibility of American involvement, then Wilson's policies at this time were unwise. This generalization, however, is faulty in all its assumptions. To begin with, American interests would be best served by a stalemate and by a peace of reconciliation through Wilson's mediation, not by driving the Allies into sullen opposition, thereby making mediation impossible, and not by promoting a German victory. More important was the fact that implementing the *modus vivendi* would not have prevented the conflict with Germany that Wilson wished to avoid. As we now know, and as Wilson did not know, conflict would come inevitably when the Germans had enough submarines to institute an effective blockade. In that event neither right nor law nor concessions by the United States would dissuade the Germans from making an all-out bid for victory through a devastating attack upon all maritime commerce to the Allied nations.

With the conclusion of the *Sussex* crisis, Wilson's task of erecting a solid structure of neutral policies to govern

relations with Britain and Germany was complete, and
the next great effort of American foreign policy would be
aimed at the higher goal of peace. Operating within the
limitations imposed by American public opinion, external
realities, and his own conception of the right role for the
United States to play, Wilson had made the only kind of
adjustments possible in view of American rights and
duties as the leading neutral power. He was now in a
position from which he could launch his peace campaign.
Thus by virtue of Wilson's leadership, American neutrality
was not merely a fact in the spring of 1916, but the most
important and the most hopeful fact of international life
at the time.

There remains only the question whether it was wise.
Some critics have argued that Wilson's great failure lay
actually in being too neutral, in failing to see that conflict with Germany was inevitable, in failing to prepare
the American people emotionally and physically to meet
the test of war, and in failing to throw American resources
and influence behind the Allies early in the war, in the
same way that Franklin D. Roosevelt did in 1940 and
1941.

If one remembers the domestic circumstances and realities that helped to govern the formation of the policy of
neutrality, and if one recalls that war with Germany did
not *seem* inevitable at any time before 1917, then this
criticism seems positively unreal. If one remembers Wilson's strenuous efforts to force a reluctant Congress to
expand the nation's military and naval forces, and how
he succeeded only partially because of popular opposition,
then the criticism seems unfair. If one agrees that American interests, indeed, the interests of mankind, would
have been best served by a peace based upon the inability
of either side to impose sweeping terms, then the criticism
seems also shallow.

CHAPTER III

WILSON *and the decisions for war*

THE INTERVAL BETWEEN May 1, 1916, and February 1, 1917, was one of the fateful turning points of modern history, because the decisions that the leaders of the great powers made during this brief period determined the future of mankind for generations to come. It was a time of gloom, because by the spring of 1916 the war had become a bloody stalemate in the trenches and upon the seas, and its futile continuation could mean only the attrition and perhaps the ruin of Western civilization. It was also a time of hope, for, as events turned out, statesmen had the opportunity to end the war on terms that might have promised a secure and peaceful future.

The story that follows is one of how Wilson and the leaders of the belligerent governments made the decisions that would determine whether the war should end or proceed, and whether the United States should remain neutral or be forced to throw in its lot with one side or the other. I will tell this story not in terms of the chronology of the events that transpired during these fateful months,

but in terms of the decisions that produced the awful final
outcome, the continuation of the war in all its agony for
the peoples of Europe.

Wilson made the first decision during the period under
review. It was to press for mediation under the terms of
the House-Grey Agreement, a choice almost foreordained
by developments that I described in the preceding chapter.
Indeed, he began even before the end of the *Sussex* crisis,
only to encounter a firm refusal by Sir Edward Grey, the
British Foreign Secretary, who made it plain that he preferred American belligerency and that he did not have
much hope for the President's mediation in any event.

Undaunted by these early rebuffs, Wilson, assisted by
Colonel House, returned to the task with a new zeal born
of the hope engendered by the happy resolution of the
Sussex affair and his and House's still strong belief that
the British leaders sincerely wanted peace. From May 10
through July 15, 1916, the two American leaders applied
a mounting pressure upon the British Foreign Office, appealing, pleading, and warning that British refusal to co-
operate with the President would drive the United States
into complete isolation and compel the Washington government to re-examine its attitude toward British maritime measures. As Wilson put it:

> We are plainly face to face with this alternative,
> therefore. The United States must either make a de-
> cided move for peace (upon some basis that promises
> to be permanent) or, if she postpones that, must insist
> to the limit upon her rights of trade and upon such
> freedom of the seas as international law already justi-
> fies her in insisting on as against Great Britain, with
> the same plain speaking and firmness that she has used
> against Germany. And the choice must be made im-

mediately. Which does Great Britain prefer? She cannot escape both. To do nothing is now, for us, impossible.[1]

In the beginning Grey tried to avoid a plain refusal by saying that the time for calling a peace conference was not yet ripe, and by urging the President to raise the question with the French government, which he knew would reject outright any suggestions of peace. But when pressed for a direct answer, the Foreign Secretary finally had to reply frankly that the Allies, and not the United States, would decide when the time for peace talks had come, and that there was no chance of implementing the House-Grey Agreement so long as the Allies had any hope of winning a military decision. In addition, other spokesmen of the British and French governments, who were not as much personally involved as Grey, made it plain by private conversation and public statement that the Allies would regard any mediation move by the President as a hostile act designed to deprive them of their chance of victory.

In this manner, therefore, did the Allied leaders risk the loss of American friendship and make their decision to prolong the war. It was a decision rendered all the more momentous by the fact that this was the time above all others when Wilson's mediation seemed to have some chance of being accepted by the Central Powers. In Germany the civilian leaders still had the upper hand in Imperial councils; convinced that neither the Kaiser's armies nor his submarines could break the deadlock, the authorities in Berlin were applying heavy pressure in Washington to persuade the President to take speedy and resolute steps toward peace. Surely there were some

[1] Wilson to E. M. House, May 16, 1916, the Ray Stannard Baker Collection of Wilson Materials, Library of Congress.

hopeful possibilities in this situation, but the Allied leaders were not interested in exploring them seriously.

It would, therefore, be easy to conclude that the British and French statesmen who refused to join hands with Wilson in a campaign for peace must bear a large measure of responsibility for the disasters that befell the world as a consequence of the prolongation of the war. The accusation is only partially, if at all, fair. The Allied leaders were not free agents. They were prisoners of history and made what was virtually an inevitable decision.

It was inevitable in the first place because of the wide gulf between Allied war objectives and the kind of peace settlement that President Wilson intended to propose and support at a peace conference. By 1916, Allied war objectives were such that they could only be imposed upon a beaten foe. In contrast, Wilson's whole policy, as Sir Edward Grey later characterized it, " was founded on the assumption that the war was a stalemate, and that the most useful role of the United States was to promote an honourable end without a crushing victory." [2]

Should a peace conference assemble as a consequence of implementing the House-Grey Agreement, Colonel House explained to the British leaders during the negotiations preceding the initialing of the document, the President would *probably* support some of their war aims, namely, the return of Alsace-Lorraine to France, Russian control of the Dardanelles, and the restoration of Belgium. But House never once promised that the United States would fight even for these minimum objectives; and he made it clear that the President had no desire to destroy German power in Europe, and that the Allies must be prepared to make concessions to Germany as a price for limited gains of their own. Wilson's great goal and

---

[2] Viscount Grey of Fallodon, *Twenty-Five Years*, II, 134.

the one for which he was willing to pledge the use of American power, House also made clear during the negotiations in London, was the establishment of a new security system to maintain freedom of the seas and enforce a guarantee of territorial integrity and political independence. As Grey wrote, " If either side, even Germany, were to agree with him in this, he would use the influence of the United States to bring the other side into line. His suggestion of mediation could not be confined to one side." [3]

The peace settlement that Wilson had in mind was one that the Allied governments would have been willing to accept only if their coalition were in danger of military defeat or political disintegration. The supreme Allied objectives were the defeat of Germany and the imposition of terms. As long as these objectives seemed possible of attainment, the House-Grey Agreement would not be implemented, or even be seriously considered.

A second and more compelling cause of the failure of the Agreement was the fact that peace through Wilson's mediation would have been an exceedingly hazardous undertaking for the Allies at this time, even had they been fighting merely for a settlement based upon the *status quo ante bellum*. The Germans, who occupied Belgium, northern France, and most of eastern Europe and the Balkan area, would have held all the trumps at a peace conference. The Allies were, therefore, understandably reluctant to agree to end the fighting without an iron-clad promise from Wilson that the United States would enter the war if the Germans refused to evacuate the territories they had conquered. Actually, the President never made and could not constitutionally make any such commitment; indeed, his repeated declarations to the effect that terri-

[3] *Ibid.* For further discussion of this important point see my *Woodrow Wilson and the Progressive Era* (New York, 1954), pp. 197-205.

torial issues did not concern him and that the belligerents
would have to settle such questions among themselves
could mean to the Allied leaders only that he thought
they were not worth fighting for.

There was an additional Allied fear, one so important
that it would have justified refusal to implement the
House-Grey Agreement, even had the President been willing and able to give adequate political guarantees. It was
the suspicion that even if he wanted to do so Wilson
would not be able to bring the United States into the war
in accord with the most vital condition stipulated in the
agreement, namely, if Germany proved to be " unreasonable " at the peace conference. There was, to begin with,
the danger that Wilson would be defeated in the forthcoming election and that his successor would either repudiate or ignore the agreement. In the second place, there
was the even graver danger that American public opinion
would not permit the President to fulfill his commitment
if he were re-elected. There were many signs that this
was true even when Grey and House initialed their agreement. By the time that Wilson was pressing for an execu-
tion of the instrument, the evidences of American determination to avoid participation on any grounds short of
direct attack were positively conclusive to British ob-
servers.

Finally, there was the fact that the Allied leaders knew
there was a good chance that Germany would break
the *Sussex* pledge when she had enough submarines to
establish an effective blockade of the British Isles. Such
a step, the Allied statesmen further knew, might mean
full-fledged American participation, and this in turn might
make a decisive Allied victory possible. Hence, they would
never accept American mediation so long as there seemed
to be any hope of American involvement.

In refusing Wilson's mediation during the spring and

summer of 1916, Grey and his colleagues in London and Paris were acting in the only way that circumstances permitted. As prisoners of their own ambitions, they simply could not see the course that would have promoted the long-range welfare of mankind. As men responsible for the security of their countries, they could not incur the enormous risks of mediation unaccompanied by iron-clad guarantees of American support.

Wilson's response was a decision with momentous possibilities for good or for ill—to strengthen American neutrality and then to press forward in his own independent campaign for peace. It was the grand culmination of American neutrality and the almost inevitable outgrowth of pressures and events at home and abroad that were converging during the summer and autumn of 1916 to cause a radical shift in American foreign policy.

One of these events was Wilson's mounting anger with the British and his growing disillusionment about the merits of the whole Allied cause as a consequence of the British rejection (as he saw it) of his right hand of fellowship. Going far beyond mere irritation, this anger and disillusionment culminated in convictions powerful enough to affect national policy—that the Allies were fighting for selfish motives and domination, and that they would prolong the carnage rather than consent to a fair and liberal settlement.

Developments in the official relations of the United States and Great Britain during the summer and autumn of 1916 also speeded the disillusionment in Washington and prepared the way for a change of American policy. To state the matter briefly, the Admiralty and Ministry of Blockade tightened the British maritime system to the point of denying the last vestiges of the freedom of the seas. This they did by such measures as the search and

seizure of American mail, carrying the economic war to
America by forbidding British subjects to have any deal-
ings with neutral individuals and firms suspected of trading with the Central Powers, and attempting to bring all
American shipping under British control by denying ship-
masters the right to purchase coal in distant British ports
if they refused to submit to the Admiralty's control.

A force of even greater power propelling Wilson toward
policies of stern neutrality and independent mediation
was the extraordinary growth of American neutralism following the settlement of the *Sussex* affair. In part it was
the result of a sharp increase in anti-British sentiment as a
consequence of the tightening of the maritime system and
the American revulsion against the ruthless way in which
the British army suppressed the Irish Rebellion in April,
1916. In larger measure it was a reflection of the overwhelming desire to avoid participation in a war the outcome of which did not concern most Americans. Whatever
the causes for its spectacular increase, neutralism became
the reigning passion during the summer and autumn of
1916. It silenced most interventionists and destroyed
politically the few (like Theodore Roosevelt) who refused
to acknowledge its supremacy, invaded the national political conventions and controlled the writing of the party
platforms, and made captives of both Wilson and his
Republican opponent, Charles Evans Hughes, during the
presidential campaign. Most important, it convinced Wilson that the vast majority of Americans would prefer
to yield technically legal rights rather than to fight if
Germany violated the *Sussex* pledge.

There was a final and irresistible force propelling Wilson
toward a new diplomatic course at this time—his fear that
the war was entering a new and more desperate stage in
which the aggressions of the belligerents might drive the
American people to war in sheer anger. If this happened,

then Americans would be fighting in blind defense of national rights, not knowing really why they fought, and only to the end that one side might win a smashing victory and thus be able to impose a peace that could not endure. The President explained the possible dilemma poignantly in a draft of a peace note that he composed in November, 1916, but did not send:

> The position of neutral nations . . . has been rendered all but intolerable. Their commerce is interrupted, their industries are checked and diverted, the lives of their people are put in constant jeopardy, they are virtually forbidden the accustomed highways of the sea. . . . If any other nation now neutral should be drawn in, it would know only that it was drawn in by some force it could not resist, because it had been hurt and saw no remedy but to risk still greater, it might be even irreparable, injury, in order to make the weight in the one scale or the other decisive; and even as a participant it would not know how far the scales must tip before the end would come or what was being weighed in the balance! [4]

It was to avoid being caught in such a predicament as this that Wilson embarked upon the policies that I will now describe.

First, he began to move in a really menacing way to defend alleged American neutral rights in the face of the new British maritime measures. No longer couched in friendly terms, the State Department's protests now accused the London government of " lawless " conduct and warned that the United States would not tolerate the continuation of " repeated violations of international law." To give teeth to these warnings, Wilson obtained legislation from Congress in early September empowering him

---

[4] From the draft printed in R. S. Baker, *Woodrow Wilson: Life and Letters* (8 vols.; Garden City, N. Y., 1927–1939), VI, 382.

to deny clearance and port facilities to ships of any nation that discriminated against American commerce, and to use the armed forces to enforce the prohibition. In addition, he persuaded the Federal Reserve Board to warn American bankers to exercise caution in financing the war trade with the Allies.

The consequences of this new sternness—a sharp increase in Anglo-American tension and vigorous protests from London—were also a calculated component of Wilson's plan. His grand objective was independent mediation, and such mediation would be possible only from a posture of severe neutrality. In other words, mediation could succeed only if the President convinced the British that he meant to use his powers of retaliation to force them to co-operate, and the Germans that he was determined to compel as much respect for American rights from their enemies as he had from them.

Wilson proceeded with his preparations for a climactic peace campaign once the voters had decreed that he should have charge of foreign relations for another four years. Protracted discussions among Wilson, Lansing, and House during late November, 1916, pointed up the possibilities and dangers of the situation. The Allies were now even more violently opposed to peace talk of any kind than they had been during the preceding summer. The German leaders, on the other hand, were not only increasing their pressure on Wilson for a peace move, but were now even promising (at least so the German Ambassador in Washington said) to evacuate Belgium and France if the Allies consented to an armistice. There was the danger, therefore, as House and Lansing pointed out, that Germany would respond favorably to a call for peace and that the Allies would reject it. If this happened, the President's advisers further warned, then the United States might drift into a sympathetic alliance with Germany and into a naval war with England and Japan. Would it not be safer, House asked, to attempt to revive the House-Grey Agreement and to move for mediation under its terms?

These were weighty issues, and in dealing with them Wilson revealed for the first time his innermost thoughts about the war and America's duty toward the belligerents. Old plans like the House-Grey Agreement based upon the assumption of intimate Anglo-American co-operation were, he exclaimed, out of date. He must stand for peace alone, free and compelling, no matter what the risks might be. If the Germans responded favorably, he would work with them. If the Allies resisted, he would attempt to coerce them. There was the risk of a rupture and war, but he did not think that it was great.

"This morning in discussing these matters with the President," House wrote in his Diary on November 15, 1916,

> he went so far as to say that if the Allies wanted war with us we would not shrink from it. . . . He thought they would not dare resort to this and if they did, they could do this country no serious hurt. I disagreed with him again. I thought Great Britain might conceivably destroy our fleet and land troops from Japan in sufficient numbers to hold certain parts of the United States. He replied they might get a good distance but would have to stop somewhere.

Neither these somber warnings, which he did not take seriously, nor the call by the German government for a peace conference, issued on December 12, diverted Wilson from the course that he had decided to pursue, and he sent a message to the belligerent capitals on December 18, 1916. In order to avoid the appearance of supporting the German maneuver, the President eliminated a demand

for the assembling of a peace conference and simply asked
the belligerents to say frankly what they were fighting
for and upon what terms they would consent to end the
war. The whole world knew, however, that it was merely
the first step in a bold campaign.

The time was now at hand when the belligerent leaders
had to choose between peace and prolonging the war at the
risk of incurring American intervention. To provide the
opportunity for frank discussions, Wilson opened secret
negotiations through Colonel House with the British Ambassador in Washington, with Sir William Wiseman, an
agent accredited to the British Embassy, and with the
German Ambassador to the United States. While waiting
for their replies, moreover, the President went before the
Senate on January 22, 1917, to describe the kind of settlement that he hoped to achieve.

The British gave their answer first, on January 26, 1917,
when Wiseman told House that his government would
agree to the meeting of an early peace conference, provided that the Germans returned a favorable reply to the
President's appeal. It was a startling announcement in
view of the hitherto bitter opposition of the British Cabinet
to any suggestion of mediation and the Allied public
answer of January 10, 1917, to Wilson's peace note, which
had revealed ambitions so sweeping that they could be
realized only by the defeat of Germany. We can only
guess at the reasons behind Wiseman's reply until the
Foreign Office in London unseals its records for this period.
By the beginning of 1917 the British almost certainly knew
that the Germans had decided to begin unrestricted submarine operations in the near future. It is possible, therefore, that the leaders in London were buying Wilson's good
will cheaply by giving lip service to the cause of peace in
the knowledge that the United States would soon be safely

in the war. It is also possible that the British had concluded that the risks of Wilsonian mediation were less than the risks of defeat through an effective submarine blockade and the disintegration of the Great Alliance, both of which now seemed ominously possible.

At this point, however, it mattered comparatively little what the British said, or why they said it. Wilson had the power of life or death over the Allies and was prepared to use it to force them to the peace table, provided that the Germans approved his objectives and accepted his leadership. As he put it:

> If Germany really wants peace she can get it, and get it soon, *if she will but confide in me and let me have a chance.* . . . Feelings, exasperations are neither here nor there. Do they want me to help? I am entitled to know because I genuinely want to help and have now put myself in a position to help without favour to either side.[5]

In the circumstances prevailing during the late autumn and early winter of 1916–1917, the Germans had three possible choices of policy. These were, first, to join hands with Wilson in a drive for peace generally on the President's terms; second, to make a limited bid for victory by intensifying the submarine war at the risk of alienating the United States; and, third, to make a supreme bid for victory by instituting a total blockade of all commerce to the British Isles. The situation from the German point of view was such that this choice would not depend upon anything that Wilson did or said, unless, of course, the President could be used as a German pawn or was willing openly to support Germany's war objectives. The German decision would depend entirely upon a realistic evaluation

[5] Wilson to E. M. House, January 24, 1917, R. S. Baker Collection, Library of Congress.

of the possibilities of the military situation, that is, upon whether the Imperial army and navy were capable of imposing terms upon the enemies of the Reich.

Discussions of these possibilities had begun in Germany in earnest in mid-August, 1916, as a consequence of the urgent demand of the Admiralty for permission to resume unrestricted submarine attacks in the near future. The civilian and military leaders rejected the demand at a conference at Pless Castle on August 31, 1916, on the ground that the navy did not have enough submarines to enforce a blockade and that it would obviously be foolhardy to risk American retaliation at this time. Actually, it was the new commanders of the army, Generals Paul von Hindenburg and Erich von Ludendorff, who made this decision. The military situation, they said, was too menacing to justify assuming the risk of war with America. There was heavy Allied pressure on the western front; above all, there was the grave danger of an Allied invasion of the Balkans, which might cause the collapse of Austria-Hungary.

Events of the late summer and early autumn combined inexorably to create a new situation in which a different decision would be made. First, the great British offensive on the Somme, aimed at tearing a huge hole in the German lines and a thrust into Belgium, failed; as a result, the German position in the West was again secure. Second, after dawdling in the matter for nearly two years, the Admiralty had finally launched a large program of submarine construction and the training of crews; by the end of the year it would be possible to talk in terms of dealing England a deathblow underseas. Finally, the army's counteroffensive against the Russians and its smashing victory over Rumania removed all cause for concern about the security of Austria-Hungary and the Balkans.

It was amid increasingly hopeful circumstances, therefore, that the German leaders, during November and early December, 1916, began to review their decision to hold the U-boats within the limits of the *Sussex* pledge. By this time Hindenburg and Ludendorff had concluded that the army could not break the stalemate on land and that the only hope of victory was an effective submarine blockade of the British Isles. On the other hand, the civilian leaders, particularly the Imperial Chancellor, Theobald von Beth-mann-Hollweg, were still convinced that a submarine *démarche* would not only fail, but would insure Germany's ultimate defeat, because it would drive the United States to hostilities. Maneuvering within a narrowing confine of authority, the Chancellor countered with the one suggestion that offered any hope of averting a break with the United States—that the Central Powers try to end the war by negotiation. The High Command agreed, but warned that the inauguration of unrestricted submarine warfare would have to follow if the peace move failed. This, in brief, was the background of the German peace note of December 12, 1916.

As we have seen, American and German policies seemingly converged at this moment. The German leaders, even the Supreme High Command, sincerely wanted peace; the President was willing to risk his leadership and the fortunes of his country by forcing the Allies to come to a peace conference. Why, then, did what seemed almost inevitable—German-American co-operation in a peace campaign—never materialize?

The answer is not to be found by suggesting that the chief cause of the failure was Wilson's refusal to move more quickly or more forcefully. There is no reason to believe that the outcome would have been any different had the President made his peace appeal in early November or in any stronger language than he later used. The answer can be found only in a clear understanding of what the Germans hoped to gain through peace negotiations and the part that they wanted Wilson to play in the final processes.

Almost formless at the outset of the war, German war objectives had grown in a direct ratio to the progress of the Imperial armies in the field. By the late autumn of 1916 the military situation was so favorable and the potentialities of an effective submarine blockade were so great that the German leaders inevitably abandoned thought of a compromise peace and began to plan for a settlement that would remove all threats to future German security. As drawn up by Bethmann-Hollweg, amended by Hindenburg, and approved by the German and Austrian governments, the German peace terms were breathtaking in scope. They included, in the East, the establishment of a Polish kingdom under German control and German annexation of Lithuania and Courland on the Baltic; in the West, destruction of British naval supremacy, an indemnity from England and France, the annexation of strategic parts of France and Belgium, and the reconstruction of Belgium as a German vassal; and, overseas, the annexation of all or part of the Belgian Congo. To be sure, these were the maximum German objectives at the time; a realization of even part of them, however, would have secured German domination of Europe for years to come.

This was the kind of settlement that the German leaders were determined to obtain through peace negotiations. They knew that they could never obtain such terms, or even a large part of them, through Wilson's mediation. They knew that Wilson would demand, among other things, the restitution of a free and independent Belgium and perhaps the return of Alsace-Lorraine to France. Acceptance of Wilson's mediation and a compromise peace, even one based entirely upon the *status quo ante bellum*, would, in German eyes, be tantamount to defeat, for it would mean the frustration of everything for which so much German blood had been shed. As a consequence, no German leader, civilian or military, ever seriously considered accepting Wilson's *mediation*. During all the high-level discussions about peace plans, no German leader ever seriously mentioned such a possibility. On the contrary, all German diplomatic efforts were concentrated upon the goal of preventing Wilson's mediation, or " meddling," as the Germans called it.

This statement needs some clarification. The Germans were eager, almost desperately eager, to win the President's support for their peace plans. They wanted Wilson's help in forcing the Allies to the peace table at a time when all the odds favored the winning of a German peace. They were willing to give pledges of postwar disarmament and membership in a League of Nations, if this were necessary to win the President's support. But they did not want, indeed, they would not permit, Wilson's mediation or even his presence at the peace conference.

Wilson did not know these facts during the first stages of the peace discussions, but the truth finally came out in January, 1917, when the President begged the Foreign Office in Berlin to come out frankly and fully in acceptance of his mediation. Then the German leaders had to say that they would welcome Wilson's co-operation only after the peace treaty had been signed, not at the conference of belligerents itself. Shrewdly perceiving the German intentions, Wilson refused to be a pawn in Berlin's game.

Wilson's refusal meant that the German leaders would now proceed to consider means of achieving through force what they had failed to win by their inept diplomacy. The High Command had already made the decision by late December; it was confirmed by a conference of all leaders at Pless Castle on January 9, 1917. That decision was, in brief, to begin unrestricted submarine warfare against all shipping, belligerent and neutral, in the approaches to the British Isles and the eastern Mediterranean after January 31.

It was easily the most fateful decision made by any government during the course of the war, and the German records fully reveal the reasons for its adoption. It now seemed beyond all doubt that the navy had sufficient power to establish an effective submarine blockade of the British Isles, for it could send between twenty-five and thirty submarines into western waters by February 1, 1917, and a growing number after that date. Moreover, other circumstances, particularly a short wheat crop in the New World, augured well for the success of the blockade. Indeed, on a basis of elaborate calculations the Admiralty spokesmen guaranteed absolutely to reduce the British to actual starvation within five months after the submarine blockade began. If this were possible, then Germany had it within her power to win a total victory and a settlement that would establish the Reich in an unassailable position. To the military leaders, who had despaired of winning the war in the trenches, it was an opportunity that could not be refused.

Fear of American belligerency no longer had any effect on German policy in such an atmosphere of confident expectation. The German leaders all assumed that a wholesale attack on American maritime commerce would drive the United States into the war. These same leaders also concluded that American belligerency would not make any difference. On the contrary, American participation would have certain positive advantages, for it would mean the diversion of huge quantities of food and matériel to an American army in training during the very period when the U-boats would be winning the war on the seas. But in any event, American participation was in the circumstances necessary to the success of the German plans, because the submarine blockade could succeed only if it were total, that is, only if American as well as British ships were prevented from carrying life-giving supplies to the beleaguered British Isles. Of course, no German leader wanted recklessly to provoke an American declaration of war; all Germans, however, were prepared to incur American belligerency if they could win the war by so doing.

It was the only decision that seemed possible to the Imperial military commanders. No nation involved in a desperate war for survival will fail to use a weapon, whether it be the submarine or the atomic bomb, when that weapon promises to bring quick and overwhelming victory. But the submarine campaign brought catastrophic defeat to Germany and misfortunes unnumbered to the world because it destroyed all possibility of a peace of reconciliation. For this outcome, the political leaders in Berlin, particularly Chancellor Bethmann-Hollweg, were primarily responsible. Not once during the critical months of 1916 did they attempt to organize any movement for peace on a basis that could succeed. Not once did the Foreign Office make any serious effort to understand Wilson's motives and objectives. Not once during the final debates over submarine policy did the Chancellor attempt to subject the Admiralty's dubious promises to any really searching scrutiny, to determine in a realistic way what the effect of American participation would be, or to inform the Reichstag of the consequences of failure of unlimited underseas warfare. It is true that the Supreme High Command, which now had the constitutional right to override the Chancellor on submarine policy, might have proceeded as it did in any event. None the less, the fact remains that Bethmann-Hollweg simply made no serious effort to influence what was the most fateful decision confronting Germany's leaders since the formation of the Empire.

There remains only one further question, whether the Germans decided to go the whole length and to attack American shipping because they believed that the United States would enter the war in any case if they violated the *Sussex* pledge. In other words, did the Germans conclude that there was little point in confining unrestricted attacks to armed merchantment or to *belligerent* shipping, armed and unarmed, because any deviations from the rules of cruiser warfare would provoke American intervention? This is an academic question, but an important one, because the answer to it sheds additional light upon Wilson's intentions and the German choice of alternatives.

There is much evidence that by the end of 1916 Wilson was prepared to effect a sharp diplomatic withdrawal if both belligerent groups refused to heed his peace appeal. He knew that if the war proceeded the belligerents would use every means at their command to end it, and that this would mean a severe intensification of the struggle on the seas, to the further detriment of neutral rights. It seems almost certain that he would have accepted unrestricted submarine attacks against *armed* merchantmen. On January 10, 1917, the German government informed the State Department that its submarines would hereafter attack armed merchant ships without warning, because these ships had all been offensively armed and instructed to attack submarines. The German proclamation was, technically, a violation of the *Sussex* pledge, but Wilson's only response was to indicate that he doubted that his earlier position on armed ships had been sound.

We can go further and say that it seems also possible that Wilson would not have broken diplomatic relations over unrestricted submarine attacks against all *belligerent* merchantmen, exclusive, perhaps, of passenger liners.

Much would have depended upon American public opinion, which then seemed overwhelmingly opposed to war for the vindication of the right of Americans to travel on belligerent vessels. Much would have depended upon the President himself, but his determination to avoid participation had never been stronger than at this time. " There will be no war," he told Colonel House on January 4, 1917.

> This country does not intend to become involved in this war. We are the only one of the great white nations that is free from war to-day, and it would be a crime against civilization for us to go in.

The Germans never seriously considered adopting these limited alternatives, not because they believed that any infraction of the *Sussex* pledge would automatically provoke American intervention, but because they thought that they could win only by enforcing a total blockade. But if it is true that Wilson would not have gone to war if the Germans had confined their attacks to belligerent merchantmen, then we are confronted with one of the supreme ironies of history. By doing the thing that seemed the best guarantee of victory, the Germans assured their own defeat. By failing to adopt the limited policies, they threw away their one chance of success, which might well have come after the collapse of Russia and a devastating attack on Allied commerce.

President Wilson's response to the German blockade proclamation lends additional evidence to my theory that the United States might not have broken diplomatic relations if the Germans had exempted American shipping from the wrath of their underseas campaign. The German Ambassador delivered copies of the German blockade announcement to Lansing and House on January 31, 1917. Wilson did not act like a man who had a predetermined course of action in mind. Even in the face of a German declaration of war against American commerce, he hesitated to take any step that might lead to war. He was willing, he told Lansing, to go to almost any lengths " rather than to have this nation actually involved in the conflict."

There was, however, only one decision that Wilson could now make. No great power could continue to maintain diplomatic intercourse with a government that promised to destroy its shipping and slaughter its citizens in violation of national and treaty rights and solemn pledges. Small neutral states like Holland and Norway had no choice but to suffer under protest, but a great nation like the United States had responsibilities commensurate with its power and influence. Continuing to maintain relations with Berlin after the issuance of the blockade proclamation of January 31 would have meant nothing less than Wilson's condoning of the German assault upon American rights and lives. The remarkable thing is not that Wilson severed diplomatic relations as he did on February 3, but that he hesitated at all.

To engage in a debate at this point over the reasons for Wilson's severance of diplomatic relations with Germany would obscure a development that was vastly more important than the handing of passports to the German Ambassador. It was Wilson's announcement, made in an address to Congress on February 3, 1917, that the United States would accept the new submarine blockade and would not go to war, in spite of the break in relations, provided that the Germans did not carry out their threat to destroy American ships and lives. This is the clear meaning of the following paragraph in Wilson's address:

Notwithstanding this unexpected action of the German Government, . . . I refuse to believe that it is the intention of the German authorities to do in fact what they have warned us they will feel at liberty to do. I cannot bring myself to believe that they will indeed pay no regard to the ancient friendship between their people and our own or to the solemn obligations which have been exchanged between them and destroy *American ships and take the lives of American citizens* in the wilful prosecution of the ruthless naval programme they have announced their intention to adopt. Only actual overt acts on their part can make me believe it even now.

Wilson then announced what he would do in the event that his confidence in the " sobriety and prudent foresight " of the German leaders proved unfounded:

I shall take the liberty of coming again before the Congress, to ask that authority be given me to use any means that may be necessary for the protection of our seamen and our people in the prosecution of their peaceful and legitimate errands on the high seas.[6]

In short, Wilson was saying that he would follow a policy of watchful waiting and govern his future policies in response to what the Germans did. If they spared American ships and lives, presumably upon American ships of all categories and upon belligerent unarmed passenger vessels, then he would do nothing. If they attacked American ships, then he would defend them by an armed neutrality. This, obviously, was not the language of war, such as Lansing had urged the President to use. It was the language of a man determined to avoid such full-fledged commitment as a war declaration would imply,

[6] Ray S. Baker and William E. Dodd (eds.), *The Public Papers of Woodrow Wilson, The New Democracy* (2 vols.; New York, 1926), ii, 425. Italics added.

willing in the worst event only to protect " our seamen and our people in the prosecution of their peaceful and legitimate errands on the high seas."

Throughout the first weeks of February, 1917, the President waited patiently to see what the future would bring. At any moment the German government could have removed the possibility of war with the United States by declaring that it would respect American shipping and take all possible care to protect American lives on belligerent ships. But when the Swiss Minister in Washington offered to serve as an intermediary in any discussions between Berlin and Washington, the German Foreign Office replied that not even the re-establishment of diplomatic relations with the United States would prompt the Imperial government to reconsider " its resolution to completely stop by submarines all importations from abroad by its enemies."

In spite of the obvious German determination to enforce a total blockade, Wilson refused to permit the defense departments to make any important preparations for war. He would not do anything to cause the Germans to think that he was contemplating hostilities. As the days passed, however, the pressures for an end to watchful waiting and for the adoption of at least an armed neutrality mounted almost irresistibly. Members of the Cabinet, shipowners, a large majority of the newspapers, and a growing body of public opinion combined in the demand that the President either convoy merchantmen or arm them with naval guns and crews. Still protesting that the people wanted him to avert any risk of war, Wilson gave in to their wishes on about February 25. Going to Congress the following day to request authority to arm merchantmen and to " employ any other instrumentalities or methods that may be necessary and adequate to protect our ships and our people in their legitimate and peaceful pursuits on the seas," he carefully explained that he was not contemplating war or any steps that might lead to war. " I merely request," he said,

> that you will accord me by your own vote and definite bestowal the means and the authority to safeguard in practice the right of a great people who are at peace and who are desirous of exercising none but the rights of peace to follow the pursuits of peace in quietness and good will—rights recognized time out of mind by all the civilized nations of the world. No course of my choosing or of theirs will lead to war. War can come only by the wilful acts and agressions of others.[7]

Although a small group of senators prevented approval of a bill authorizing Wilson to arm merchantmen, the President took such action anyway on March 9, 1917. At the same time, he called Congress into special session for April 16, 1917, presumably in order to ask the legislative branch to sanction a more elaborate program of armed neutrality, which he set to work with his advisers in the Navy Department to devise.

By the middle of March, therefore, it seemed that Wilson had made his decision in favor of a limited defensive war on the seas. " We stand firm in armed neutrality," he declared, for example, in his second inaugural address on March 5, " since it seems that in no other way we can demonstrate what it is we insist upon and cannot forego." Yet on April 2 (he had meanwhile convened Congress for this earlier date), scarcely more than a month after he had uttered these words, he stood before Congress and asked for a declaration of full-fledged war. What events occurred, what forces were at work, what pressures were applied during this brief interval to cause Wilson to make the decision that he had been trying so desperately to

[7] *Ibid.*, pp. 428-32.

avoid? We should perhaps put the question in a less positive way, as follows: What caused the President to abandon armed neutrality and to *accept* the decision for war?

There was first the fact that from the end of February to the end of March the Germans gave full evidence of their determination to press a relentless, total attack against all ships passing through the war zones that enveloped western Europe. The sinking of the British liner *Laconia* without warning on February 25 and with loss of American life, the ruthless destruction of three American merchantmen (*City of Memphis, Illinois,* and *Vigilancia*) on March 18, and the relentless attacks against the vessels of other neutral nations, to say nothing of the slashing attacks against Allied merchant shipping, removed all doubt in Wilson's mind about the deadly seriousness of the German intention to conduct total warfare against all commerce and human life within the broad war zones.

The more the character of the submarine blockade became apparent, the stronger the conviction grew in the President's mind that armed neutrality was neither a sufficient response physically, nor a proper or legally possible one. He explained this conviction in his war message:

> It is a war against all nations. . . . The challenge is to all mankind. When I addressed the Congress on the 26th of February last, I thought that it would suffice to assert our neutral rights with arms, our right to use the seas against unlawful interference, our right to keep our people safe against unlawful violence. But armed neutrality, it now appears, is impracticable. Because submarines are in effect outlaws when used as the German submarines have been used against merchant shipping, it is impossible to defend ships against their attacks as the law of nations has assumed that merchantmen would defend themselves. . . . It is common prudence in such circumstances, grim necessity indeed, to endeavour to destroy them before they show their

own intention. They must be dealt with upon sight, if dealt with at all. The German Government denies the right of neutrals to use arms at all within the areas of the sea which it has proscribed, even in the defense of rights which no modern publicist has ever before questioned their right to defend. The intimation is conveyed that the armed guards which we have placed on our merchant ships will be treated as beyond the pale of law and subject to be dealt with as pirates would be. Armed neutrality is ineffectual enough at best; in such circumstances and in the face of such pretensions it is worse than ineffectual; it is likely only to produce what it was meant to prevent; it is practically certain to draw us into the war without either the rights or the effectiveness of belligerents.[8]

This passage, in my opinion, reveals the *immediate* reason why Wilson made his decision for war. It was simply that the German assault upon American lives and property was so overwhelming and so flagrant that the only possible way to cope with it was to claim the status of a belligerent in order to strike at the sources of German power. " I would be inclined to adopt . . . [armed neutrality]," the President wrote only two days before he delivered his war message,

indeed, as you know, I had already adopted it, but this is the difficulty: . . . To make even the measures of defense legitimate we must obtain the status of belligerents.[9]

Certainly Wilson had convinced himself that this was true, but I have a strong suspicion that he would have stood doggedly by his first decision to limit American

[8] *Papers Relating to the Foreign Relations of the United States, 1917, Supplement 1, The World War* (Washington, 1931), pp. 196-97.
[9] Wilson to Matthew Hale, March 31, 1917, Wilson Papers, Library of Congress.

action to a defense of rights on the seas if this decision had not been overridden by convictions, events, pressures, and ambitions that were themselves decisive in Wilson's final shift from armed neutrality to war, in forcing him to the conclusion that the *immediate* circumstances left the United States with no choice but full-scale participation.

One of the most important of these factors was the subtlest and the one for which the least direct evidence can be adduced. It was Wilson's apparent fear that the threat of a German victory imperiled the balance of power and all his hopes for the future reconstruction of the world community. We must be careful here not to misinterpret his thoughts and motives. There is little evidence that he accepted the decision for war because he thought that a German victory would seriously endanger American security, because he wanted to preserve Anglo-American control of the North Atlantic sea lanes, or because he desired to maintain the traditional balance of European power because it served American interests. Nor is there any convincing evidence that Wilson's attitude toward the objectives of the rival alliances had changed by the time that he made his final decision.

On the other hand, there was now a great and decisive difference in the relative position of the belligerents: The Allies seemed about to lose the war and the Central Powers about to win it. This, almost certainly, was a governing factor in Wilson's willingness to think in terms of war. Germany, he told Colonel House, was a madman who must be curbed. A German victory meant a peace of domination and conquest; it meant the end of all of Wilson's dreams of helping to build a secure future.

As the President pondered America's duty at this juncture in history, the answer must have seemed obvious to him—to accept belligerency, because now only through belligerency could the United States fulfill its mission to insure a just and lasting peace of reconciliation. This could be accomplished only by preventing a German victory and only by the assertion of such power and influence among the Allies as would come to the United States by virtue of its sacrifice of blood and treasure.

If the immediate events made a war resolution necessary, then the goal of a righteous peace was the objective that justified full-scale participation in Wilson's mind and raised that effort to a high and noble plane. It was, therefore, not war in anger that he advocated, not war sheerly in defense of national rights, but, as he put it in his war message,

> [war] for democracy, for the right of those who submit to authority to have a voice in their own governments, for the rights and liberties of small nations, for a universal dominion of right by such a concert of free peoples as shall bring peace and safety to all nations and make the world itself at last free.

The combined weight of official and public opinion was another pressure meanwhile driving Wilson toward acceptance of the decision for war. It was a fact of no little consequence that by the end of March every important member of the administration, including those members of the Cabinet who had heretofore opposed any bellicose measures, urged the President to admit that a state of war with Germany in fact existed. Public opinion had remained stubbornly pacific until near the end of February, 1917. Then the publication of the Zimmermann telegram, in which the German government proposed to Mexico a war alliance against the United States, the sinking of the *Laconia*, and, above all, the destruction of American ships in the war zones after mid-March generated a demand for war that grew with mounting cre-

scendo in all sections and among all classes, until it seemed
beyond doubt to be a national and a majority demand.
It was further stimulated by news of the downfall of the
czarist regime and the establishment of a provisional republican government in Russia—news that convinced
many wavering Americans that the Allies were indeed
fighting for democracy and also changed overnight the
large and influential American Jewish community from a
position of strong hostility toward the Allies to one of
friendship.

This was all a development of profound importance
for a leader as keenly sensitive to public opinion as was
Woodrow Wilson. He could have joined forces with the
large antiwar minority to resist the demand for war; indeed, he probably would have done so had he been convinced that it was the wise and right thing to do. The
point is not, therefore, that public opinion *forced* Wilson
to accept the decision for war, but that it facilitated doing
what Wilson for other reasons now thought was necessary
and right to do.

All this is said without any intention of implying that
Wilson ever *wanted* war. The agony of his soul was great
as he moved through the dark valley of his doubts. He
had no illusions about the merits of the conflict into which
he and his people were being drawn. He saw the risks of
intervention, both to his own nation and to the world,
with remarkable clarity. But he could devise no alternative; and he set aside his doubts in the hope that acting
now as a belligerent, with all the power and idealism of
the American people sustaining him, he could achieve
objectives to justify the misery of mankind.

⎰

CHAPTER IV

WILSON *and the liberal peace program*

NEVER BEFORE HAD the tasks of leadership in foreign affairs been so difficult for Woodrow Wilson as they were after the adoption of the war resolution by Congress on April 6, 1917. There was the task of articulating the war aims of the American people and of giving voice as well to the better aspirations of men everywhere without, however, driving a fatal wedge between the United States and the Allies in the war against the common foe. There was the even more arduous task after the war had ended of achieving a peace of justice and mercy in spite of the primal passions set loose by years of bloodshed and by ambitions multiplied by victory.

If the challenges were great, so also were Wilson's courage and faith during the long campaign that he waged for the ideals that he thought were the cornerstones of a lasting peace. In the following chapter I will try to describe the way in which Wilson, inspired by these ideals, worked out a peace program to free mankind from the bonds of history and the degree to which he succeeded or failed.

Nothing illustrates more clearly the functions of leadership in the great movements with which Wilson was as-

sociated than the role he played in the formulation of a
program for peace from 1916 to 1919. Not often an
originator, a pioneer, or far ahead of public opinion, he
made his chief contributions by synthesizing thought and
ideals, by expressing them in language that moved the
hearts and influenced the votes of men, and by devising
the practical means of putting these ideals to work. So it
was with Wilson's relation to the liberal peace program.
Its basic planks had already been conceived and thoroughly debated by antiwar groups in Europe and the
United States by the time that Wilson publicly espoused
their program.

Although they worked separately in different countries,
these international liberals drew upon common Christian
and humanitarian traditions and proposed virtually the
same plans for a peace settlement and postwar reconstruction. First, all liberals proposed an end to the system
of entangling alliances, balances of power, and secret
diplomacy that they were certain had helped make war
inevitable. In the place of the old methods they proposed
a concert of power for peace through open diplomacy
democratically controlled. " The foreign policy of Great
Britain," the platform of the British Union of Democratic Control read, for example,

 shall not be aimed at creating alliances for the purpose
 of maintaining the ' balance of power,' but shall be
 directed to the establishment of a concert of the powers
 and the setting up of an international council whose
 deliberations and decisions shall be public.

Or, to cite another example, the American Socialist Party
demanded that the declaration of " offensive war " should
be made " only by direct vote of the people."

Second, all international liberals were convinced that
the existence of large armies and navies was a prime cause

of conflict. Thus they urged sweeping reductions in armaments, until each nation had only such military forces as were necessary to maintain internal security. Some of the peace organizations, like the Woman's Peace Party of the United States, also demanded the nationalization of the manufacture of armaments; others, like the International Peace Bureau of Belgium, proposed strict international control. In addition, most of them suggested the internationalization of waterways like the Panama, Suez, and Kiel canals and of strategic points like Gibraltar and the Bosporus.

Third, most liberals envisaged the creation of some kind of international agency in the postwar era strong enough to protect its members against aggression. The South German Social Democrats, for example, proposed a confederacy of all European states and a universal alliance against aggression. But the most important suggestion of this kind came from an American group, the League to Enforce Peace, which was organized in June, 1915. Its objective was the establishment of a League of Nations binding its members to use their economic and military forces against any one of their number that went to war, or committed acts of hostility against another of the signatories, in violation of international agreements.

This, in brief, was the general structure for a new international order that the liberal groups had worked out by 1916. As a first step toward their objective, most of them demanded an end to the war by a settlement based upon the principles of no indemnities, self-determination or autonomy for minority peoples under alien rule, no transfer of territory without the consent of the people involved, and plebiscites to determine the fate of provinces like Alsace-Lorraine and Ireland. Working against fearful obstacles in the belligerent countries, these idealists were somehow making their program known throughout the

Western world; indeed, by 1916 they had started machinery that would cause the wheels of history to turn.

The wheels began to move in an important way when the President of the United States took leadership in the movement for the liberal peace program. This happened in the following manner:

Following Colonel House's exploratory peace mission to Europe in the late winter and early spring of 1915, Sir Edward Grey, the British Foreign Secretary, declared that his government might be willing to accept American mediation, provided that the United States would agree to join a postwar League of Nations committed to disarmament on land and sea and to the territorial integrity of member nations. "How much are the United States prepared to do in this direction?" Grey asked House in a letter dated September 22, 1915.

> Would the President propose that there should be a League of Nations binding themselves to side against any Power which broke a treaty . . . or which refused, in case of dispute, to adopt some other method of settlement than that of war? [1]

Grey could not have put this question to any more responsive person than Wilson. Since his youth, as his writings show, he had dreamed of an international association, a "parliament of man," based upon the American federal model. Only a few months before he received the letter from Grey cited above, moreover, Wilson had set plans in motion for the negotiation of a Pan-American Pact to bind the nations of the New World in guarantees of territorial integrity and political independence. He was not acting rashly and without thinking, therefore, when

[1] E. Grey to E. M. House, September 22, 1915, the Papers of Edward M. House, Yale University Library.

he replied at once to Grey that the United States was prepared to join such a League as the Foreign Minister had described.

Then followed in consequence House's second peace mission to Europe, the initialing of the House-Grey Agreement that provided the means for Anglo-American cooperation in mediation, the temporary alleviation of the submarine controversy with Germany, and Wilson's subsequent campaign for peace under the terms of the House-Grey Agreement. The President took the first public step in that campaign in an address before the League to Enforce Peace in Washington on May 27, 1916, by publicly confirming the promise that Grey had said was the prerequisite for American mediation.

Wilson began by announcing the end of the isolation of the United States.

> We are [he said] participants, whether we would or not, in the life of the world. The interests of all nations are our own also. We are partners with the rest. What affects mankind is inevitably our affair as well as the affair of the nations of Europe and of Asia.

The present war, he continued, could be ended and another such holocaust be prevented only by common recognition of the interdependence of nations and of the right of all peoples to freedom from the fear of aggression.

> I am sure [he concluded] that I speak the mind and wish of the people of America when I say that the United States is willing to become a partner in any feasible association of nations formed in order to realize these objects and make them secure against violation . . . [a] universal association of the nations to maintain the inviolate security of the highway of the seas for the common and unhindered use of all the nations of the world, and to prevent any war begun either con-

trary to treaty covenants or without warning and full
submission of the causes to the opinion of the world—
a virtual guarantee of territorial integrity and political
independence.[2]

Encouraged by what seemed to be a bipartisan and
nearly unanimous public approval of the league idea, Wilson next moved to the second stage in his assumption of
leadership of the liberal peace movement. This he did in
the address before the Senate on January 22, 1917, by
frankly telling the leaders of the belligerent powers that
the United States would be willing to join a League of
Nations and help maintain the peace settlement only if
that settlement vindicated the liberal ideals.

The United States, he warned at the beginning of this
address, had no interest in helping to create a new balance
of power. On the contrary, he said, " There must be, not
a balance of power, but a community of power; not organized rivalries, but an organized common peace." The
peace that must soon come should, therefore, be a negotiated settlement among equals, one without victors and
vanquished or humiliation and bitterness, for only a peace
among equals could last. Having thus enunciated one car-
dinal dogma of liberal internationalism, Wilson went on
to affirm others and to pledge again America's willingness
to join a postwar organization to preserve the peace. " I
am proposing, as it were, " he concluded,

> that the nations should with one accord adopt the doc-
> trine of President Monroe as the doctrine of the world:
> that no nation should seek to extend its polity over
> any other nation or people, . . . that all nations hence-
> forth avoid entangling alliances which would draw them
> into competitions of power. . . . These are American

[2] R. S. Baker and W. E. Dodd (eds.), *The Public Papers of Woodrow
Wilson, The New Democracy*, ii, 185, 187-88.

principles, American policies. We could stand for no others. And they are also the principles and policies of forward looking men and women everywhere, of every modern nation, of every enlightened community. They are the principles of mankind and must prevail.[3]

Wilson's role in the peace movement changed after the adoption of the American war resolution, but not his objective or even his essential methods. His objective was still the attainment of a peace of justice and reconciliation, his methods still those of a leader and spokesman of mankind who stood serenely above the passions and hatreds that rent Europe and were now beginning to consume his own people. He revealed his feelings in a hundred ways by what he thought and did and said during the seventeen months of American belligerency.

There was, first, the way in which Wilson defined the peculiar role that the United States was to play as an active participant in the fighting after entering the war. He had no desire to spare American resources and manpower, was determined to pursue the struggle to the bitter end for a crushing victory, if that proved necessary, and strongly supported all proposals for closer Allied and American military co-ordination. At the same time, he took assiduous pains to make it clear that the United States was in the war for its own reasons, fighting as an associate and not an ally of the European belligerents.

This was an important distinction, one that laid bare Wilson's fundamental thinking about the nature of the war and the role that America should play in it. He did not delude himself into thinking that the United States and the Allied powers were fighting for the same objectives. Indeed, after his and Colonel House's conversations with Arthur Balfour, the new British Foreign Secretary, in

[3] *Ibid.*, pp. 407-14.

May, 1917, the President knew many of the details of the Allied secret treaties for the division of enemy territories and colonies, and he was, if anything, more censorious than these agreements justified. But in any event he jealously guarded his freedom of action, first, by refusing even to discuss, much less to approve, the Allied war aims during the early months of the war, and, second, by making it unmistakably clear in his public addresses that the American people would fight only for the kind of settlement that he had generally described.

Wilson pressed this campaign for a liberal peace with a mounting intensity as the months passed in 1917. To begin with, he applied heavy pressure on Austria-Hungary to withdraw from the war, promising that he and the Allied leaders would insist only upon the federalization and not the destruction of that Empire. More important, in a series of addresses he made it clear to the German people that they could have peace on generous terms at any time, provided only that they depose their military masters, repudiate aims of conquest, and withdraw their armies from the conquered territories. Again and again he declared that Americans had no quarrel with the great German people and admired their accomplishments, even the Empire, desired their prosperity, and, above all, coveted their friendship in the postwar era.

" We intend no wrong against the German Empire," Wilson said, for example, on December 4, 1917,

> no interference with her internal affairs. We should deem either the one or the other absolutely unjustifiable, absolutely contrary to the principles we have professed to live by and to hold most sacred throughout our life as a nation. The people of Germany are being told by the men whom they now permit to deceive them and to act as their masters that they are fighting for the very life and existence of their Empire, a war of desperate

self-defense against deliberate aggression. Nothing could be more grossly or wantonly false. . . . We are in fact fighting for their emancipation from fear, along with our own—from the fear as well as from the fact of unjust attack by neighbors or rivals or schemers after world empire. No one is threatening the existence or the independence or the peaceful enterprise of the German Empire.[4]

There was much truth in a British contemporary's quip that Wilson sounded more like an arbitrator than a belligerent. The fact was that throughout 1917 he seems to have thought that there was some chance that the moderate forces in the Reichstag and the civilian leaders in the Imperial government would take control from Hindenburg and Ludendorff and open peace negotiations. If such an event had occurred, then Wilson almost certainly would have responded eagerly, even if Allied refusal to co-operate had resulted in a separate peace between the United States and Germany.

Actually, Wilson had no fears of any such rupture with the Allies in a showdown fight over peace terms, so great was his faith in his own ability to marshal world opinion behind a generous settlement. As he put it in the address of December 4, 1917, which I have just cited:

Statesmen must by this time have learned that the opinion of the world is everywhere wide awake and fully comprehends the issues involved. No representative of any self-governed nation will dare disregard it by attempting any . . . covenants of selfishness and compromise. . . . The congress that concludes this war will feel the full strength of the tide that runs now in the hearts and conscience of free men everywhere.[5]

[4] R. S. Baker and W. E. Dodd (eds.), *The Public Papers of Woodrow Wilson, War and Peace* (2 vols.; New York, 1927), I, 132-33; hereinafter cited as *War and Peace*.

[5] *Ibid.*, pp. 133-34.

There was, besides, the (to him) reassuring fact that the Allies were daily growing more dependent, both militarily and economically, upon the United States. This meant, Wilson wrote in a private letter to House on July 21, 1917, " When the war is over we can force them to our way of thinking, because by that time they will, among other things, be financially in our hands." [6]

Growing confidence in his own leadership, evidences of war-weariness everywhere in Europe, and signs of a strong revolt in the Reichstag against the military leadership all built up in Wilson an almost irresistible desire to take the final climactic step in the liberal peace campaign, that is, to affirm in specific terms what the American and, he hoped, the Allied peoples were fighting for and the conditions upon which they would consent to an armistice. He was strongly tempted to reply fully when Pope Benedict XV addressed a peace appeal to the belligerents on August 1, 1917, calling for an evacuation of conquered territories, mutual reparation, and a settlement of territorial questions based insofar as possible upon the wishes of the people involved. But the President answered the papal appeal only in general terms, saying that the American people had no desire for " punitive damages, the dismemberment of empires, the establishment of selfish and exclusive economic leagues," and warning that no enduring peace could come until the German military imperialists had been deposed.[7] " I have not thought it wise to say more or to be more specific," he explained to House on August 23,

because it might provoke dissenting voices from France or Italy if I should,—if I should say, for example, that

[6] R. S. Baker, *Woodrow Wilson: Life and Letters*, VII, 180.

[7] For the Pope's appeal and Wilson's reply see *Papers Relating to the Foreign Relations of the United States, 1917, Supplement 2, The World War* (2 vols.; Washington, 1932), I, 162-64, 177-79.

their territorial claims did not interest us. . . . My own feeling is that we should speak at the earliest possible moment now.[8]

From this point on the President wasted little time in preparing for the climax of his campaign. First, on September 2, 1917, he asked Colonel House to assemble a group of experts, subsequently known as The Inquiry, who should study the war aims of the belligerents and attempt to formulate America's own specific objectives. Next, late in October Wilson sent House to London and Paris to participate in inter-Allied military discussions and, incidentally, to press for agreement on war aims when the opportunity arose.

The opportunity, indeed, the necessity, came almost as soon as House arrived in London, as a result of the greatest catastrophe that had yet befallen the Allied cause—the seizure of the Russian government by the Bolsheviks on November 7, 1917. At once the new Soviet authorities appealed to the Allies to begin peace negotiations on a basis of no annexations and no indemnities. Now in Paris, House pleaded with the British and French leaders to approve a simple pronouncement of liberal war aims, as one means of persuading the Bolsheviks to maintain the common front. However, in spite of stern warnings from the White House that the American people would not fight for " any selfish aim on the part of any belligerent " and that it would be " a fatal mistake to cool the ardour of America," House failed to win the adoption even of an innocuous declaration and returned empty handed to Washington in mid-December.

Events and pressures of the next two weeks convinced Wilson and his advisers that an authoritative statement of war aims must soon be made. Having concluded an

[8] R. S. Baker, *Woodrow Wilson: Life and Letters*, viii, 231.

armistice with the Germans, the Bolsheviks pressed their
appeal for a general peace, published the secret treaties
between the czarist and the Allied governments negotiated
since the beginning of the war, and denounced the Allied
refusal to join their move for peace as proof of the most
perfidious ambitions. Speaking on Christmas day, the
Austrian Foreign Minister echoed the Bolshevik appeal
and declared that the Central Powers desired no forcible
annexations. Liberals, idealists, labor leaders, and Socialists in the United States and Great Britain were virtually
up in arms, denouncing Allied intransigence, declaring that
the time for peace had come, and demanding a frank reply
to the Russian and German overtures.

It was amid such circumstances that Wilson set to work
with Colonel House on January 4, 1918. With a long
memorandum prepared by The Inquiry as a guide, he
hammered out an address intended to appeal to the German moderates, to entice the Bolsheviks even yet to stand
by the Allies, and, above all, to avow the aspirations and
ideals for which the American people were fighting so
clearly that the Allied statesmen could not fail to understand them. The result was, of course, the Fourteen Points
address, which Wilson delivered before a joint session of
Congress on January 8, 1918.

He began by reviewing events that had transpired in
Russia only a few days before, the disruption of the
Soviet-German peace talks following the presentation of
extraordinarily severe demands by the Imperial German
representatives. It was evident, the President said, that
the German military masters were bent upon the conquest
and subjugation of the helpless Russian people. The time
had come, therefore, for the peace-loving nations to avow
their ideals and objectives, and these he proceeded to summarize in fourteen points.

On the one hand were the general points promising

open diplomacy, absolute freedom of the seas in peace and in war, " except as the seas may be closed in whole or in part by international action for the enforcement of international covenants," general disarmament, the removal (insofar as possible) of barriers to trade among nations, an absolutely impartial and open-minded settlement of colonial claims, and the establishment of a League of Nations.

On the other hand were the points relating to more specific issues. Two of these—the evacuation and restoration of Belgium and the evacuation of Russia and self-determination for the Russian people—were, like the general points, indispensable to the peace settlement. The remaining six points were presumably not quite as important, for in mentioning them Wilson said that they " should " rather than " must " be achieved. They were the evacuation of French territory and the return of Alsace-Lorraine to France, autonomy for the minority peoples of the Austro-Hungarian Empire, a readjustment of Italy's boundary to satisfy legitimate Irredentist claims, the evacuation of the Balkans and free development for the states of that region, security for Turkey, but autonomy for the subject peoples of the Ottoman Empire and internationalization of the Dardanelles, and the creation of an independent Poland with access to the sea.

Finally, there was a fifteenth point, one not listed and only implied, but as important as any of the rest—that the United States and the Allies had neither any jealousy of Germany's greatness nor any desire to injure her. As Wilson put it:

> We grudge her no achievement or distinction of learning or of pacific enterprise such as have made her record very bright and very enviable. We do not wish to injure her or to block in any way her legitimate influence of power. We do not wish to fight her either with

arms or with hostile arrangements of trade if she is willing to associate herself with us and the other peace-loving nations of the world in covenants of justice and law and fair dealing. We wish her only to accept a place of equality among the peoples of the world,—the new world in which we now live,—instead of a place of mastery.[9]

It would be almost superfluous to remark upon the impact of this pronouncement, so well known is the way in which it at once became the moral standard to which so many of the American and Allied peoples rallied and so obvious was the success that it ultimately achieved in undermining the willingness of the peoples of the Central Powers to continue the struggle. One aspect of the historic significance of the Fourteen Points address, however, has sometimes been overlooked. It was democracy's answer in its first full-dress debate with international communism. Lenin and Trotsky had appealed to the peace hunger of the world for the purpose of beginning a universal class war to destroy Western civilization in its democratic and Christian form. In contrast, Wilson had appealed for peace in the name of all that was high and holy in the democratic and Christian tradition for the purpose of saving Western civilization.

For a brief time it seemed almost as if Wilson had prompted conversations that might show a common ground for peace. Count Ottokar Czernin, the Austrian Foreign Minister, replied in a friendly address on January 24, accepting many basic points among the fourteen. In his reply, delivered on the same day, the new German Chancellor, Count Georg F. von Hertling, was evasive on the specific points, but approved most of the general ones. Wilson answered them on February 11, commending Czernin's moderation and declaring that Hertling's speech had

[9] R. S. Baker and W. E. Dodd, *War and Peace*, I, 155-62.

been double talk to mask the ambitions of Germany's military leaders. Peace, Wilson warned, could not be made by old methods and by old standards. National aspirations must be respected, for " self-determination " was the new rule of international life. The question whether peace conversations should continue, he concluded, depended upon whether the belligerents could agree upon four principles, namely, that justice should govern the settlement of all issues, that peoples should not be bartered and sold in the discredited game of balance of power, that every territorial settlement should be made for the benefit of the peoples concerned, and that all well-defined national aspirations should be accorded satisfaction insofar as possible.[10]

The brief dialogue between Washington and Berlin and Vienna came abruptly to an end on March 3, 1918, when the German High Command forced a harsh and punitive treaty upon the Bolsheviks at Brest-Litovsk. In a speech at Baltimore on April 6, Wilson confessed his disillusionment and despair. He had tried, he said, to judge Germany's purposes without hatred or vindictiveness. He still believed that the German civilian leaders wanted a peace of justice. But the action at Brest-Litovsk had revealed who Germany's masters were and left no doubt that they sought the domination of Europe. There was, therefore, but one response that the American people could make: " Force, Force to the utmost, Force without stint or limit, the righteous and triumphant Force which shall make Right the law of the world, and cast every selfish dominion down in the dust." [11]

The poignancy of Wilson's consternation at the Treaty of Brest-Litovsk becomes all the clearer when we remember what that treaty signified and portended. It meant, as many Allied leaders had argued and Wilson himself had

[10] *Ibid.*, pp. 177-84.
[11] *Ibid.*, pp. 199-202.

feared, that peace could be won only by the triumph of armies, only by smashing the power of the German military machine. This in turn meant a settlement, not negotiated among equals, but imposed by the victor—in short, a situation of the gravest difficulty and danger for the man who knew that it would be as necessary to restrain the ambitions of his friends as the usurpations of his enemies. But peace without victory seemed no longer possible after March, 1918, and Wilson accepted the choice that the German leaders had imposed—to press on relentlessly toward military victory. " The Past and the Present are in deadly grapple," he cried out on July 4, " and the peoples of the world are being done to death between them. There can be but one issue. The settlement must be final. There can be no compromise. . . . No halfway decision is conceivable." [12]

For several months after Wilson's new declaration of war it seemed that the final settlement might be written by the Central Powers. Transferring some forty divisions from the eastern front after the collapse of Russian resistance in the early weeks of 1918, the Germans finally achieved a numerical superiority on the western front. In March, 1918, they launched a gigantic offensive to knock France out of the war before the trickle of American reinforcements could turn into a mighty stream. The British and French forces reeled and retreated under the blows; but the French defenses held before Paris in mid-July. Soon afterward, with the help of an ever-growing American army, the supreme Allied commander, Marshal Ferdinand Foch, began a counteroffensive. By October 1, 1918, the combined Allied and American armies had broken the Hindenburg Line and were nearing the Belgian and

[12] *Ibid.*, p. 233.

German frontiers. Panic-stricken, General Ludendorff demanded that the Imperial government obtain an immediate armistice to give him time to withdraw his armies to new defensive positions.

The sequel is the familiar story of how the Germans appealed to Washington for an armistice on the basis of the Fourteen Points and Wilson's subsequent elaborations,[13] and of how Wilson maneuvered the German leaders into acknowledgment of defeat and acceptance of an armistice agreement that left them powerless to resume offensive operations. What is not so well known is the way in which President Wilson tried even at this late date to maintain some semblance of a German counterweight to Allied power. " It is certain," he advised Colonel House on October 28, " that too much success or security on the part of the Allies will make a genuine peace settle-

---

[13] These included the Four Supplementary Points of February 11, 1918, the Four Additional Points of July 4, 1918, and the Five Additional Points of September 27, 1918.

I have enumerated the Four Supplementary Points of February 11 in the body of the text above. The Four Additional Points of July 4 were the destruction or reduction to virtual impotence of every arbitrary power anywhere that could disturb the peace of the world, *e.g.*, the German military establishment, the settlement of every question upon the basis of the free acceptance of that settlement by the people immediately concerned, the consent of all nations to be governed in their conduct toward each other by the same principles of honor and of respect for law that governed the individual citizens of all modern states in their relations with one another, and the establishment of a peace organization that would " make it certain that the combined power of free nations will check every invasion of right and serve to make peace and justice . . . secure."

The Five Additional Points of September 27 were that equal justice should be done to all peoples in the peace settlement, that special interests should not be permitted to override the common interest, that there should be no special understandings within the general family of the League of Nations, that there should be no selfish economic combinations or any form of economic coercion within the League, except as a means of preventing aggression, and that all international agreements should be made known in their entirety to the rest of the world.

ment exceedingly difficult, if not impossible." Therefore, he wanted an armistice agreement that left the German ground forces intact, one which would, as he put it, " prevent a renewal of hostilities by Germany but which will be as moderate and reasonable as possible within those limits." [14]

The crucial question during these pre-Armistice negotiations was whether the Allied governments would agree to promise Germany to make peace upon a basis of the Fourteen Points and Wilson's later pronouncements. The President sent Colonel House to Paris in late October to force a final showdown before the collapse of German resistance had emboldened the Allied leaders into taking the peace negotiations into their own hands. From October 29 through November 4, House confronted the Allied prime ministers in a series of stormy interviews. Shrewdly and relentlessly the Colonel pressed his colleagues. When they threatened to repudiate the Fourteen Points, House countered with the warning that the President was prepared to make a separate peace; when they showed signs of yielding, he urged them to state their minimum reservations. The result was an agreement to promise Germany terms as stipulated in the Fourteen Points and Wilson's subsequent declarations, amended only by a British reservation of the right to discuss the point relating to freedom of the seas at the peace conference and a French " elucidation " providing that Germany should be required to make compensation for the civilian damages caused by her aggressions. This, together with the extensive military and naval provisions that Marshal Foch and his advisers had drawn up, was the substance of the so-called Pre-Armistice Agreement that the German representatives signed on November 11, 1918.

[14] R. S. Baker, *Woodrow Wilson: Life and Letters*, VIII, 523.

The opportunity for which Wilson had waited since 1915 was now almost at hand. No leader in history ever stood on the eve of a fateful undertaking with higher hopes or nobler ambitions; none, it seemed, ever approached his task with greater strength, for he had wrung explicit Allied approval of a solemn promise to make peace in accord with a program of his own devising.

It is not my purpose here either to write a biography of Wilson during this period or another history of the Paris Peace Conference.[15] Indeed, to tell the story in all its detail would be to obscure my objective in the balance of this lecture. That objective, simply stated, is to determine the degree to which Wilson succeeded or failed in vindicating the liberal peace program. This can best be done by describing the crucial areas of disagreement and by showing what the outcome was when Wilsonian idealism clashed with Allied ambitions.

The overshadowing necessity of the Paris conference was the devising of plans and measures to assure security for the French against future German aggression. Wilson offered safety in the hope of a Reich reformed because democratic, and in a League of Nations that would provide the machinery for preventing any aggression in the future. To the French, whose territory had been twice invaded by the Germans in less than half a century and who were still inferior in manpower and industry to their

---

[15] This might be a good point at which to acknowledge my indebtedness to several secondary works on the Paris Peace Conference. They are Paul Birdsall, *Versailles Twenty Years After* (New York, 1941); Thomas A. Bailey, *Woodrow Wilson and the Lost Peace* (New York, 1947); Louis A. R. Yates, " The United States and French Security, 1917–1921: A Study of the Treaty of Guarantee," unpublished Ph. D. dissertation, University of Southern California, 1950; and Étienne Mantoux, *The Carthaginian Peace, or The Economic Consequences of Mr. Keynes* (New York, 1952). These studies, especially the first two, provide useful and on the whole balanced summaries for the reader who does not have the time or energy to work through the enormous body of source materials on the conference.

eastern neighbor, such promises were not enough. Having lived under the shadow of the German colossus, they were determined to destroy it and by so doing to assure a peaceful Europe. Thus Georges Clemenceau, the French Premier, following plans devised by Marshal Foch and approved even before the United States entered the war, proposed to tear the west bank of the Rhine from Germany by the creation of one or more autonomous Rhenish republics under French control.

Arguing that the dismemberment of Germany in the West would outrageously violate the Pre-Armistice Agreement and create a wound on the body of the world community that would fester for generations to come, Wilson opposed this plan with grim determination during long and violent debates with the French spokesmen. The tension reached a climax during late March and early April, 1919, when Clemenceau accused Wilson of being pro-German and the President ordered his ship, the *George Washington*, to prepare to take him back to the United States. Some agreement, obviously, was a compelling necessity; without it the conference would have failed entirely, and the French would have been at liberty to execute their own plans in their own way.

In the showdown it was the French who made the vital concessions, by yielding their demands for the creation of the Rhenish republics and the permanent French occupation of the Rhineland. In return, Wilson and David Lloyd George, the British Prime Minister, who gave the President important support on this issue, agreed to permit a fifteen-year occupation of the Rhineland and signed with Clemenceau treaties promising that the United States and Great Britain would come to the aid of France if she were attacked by Germany. These concessions saved the conference from actual disruption. Coupled with provisions for the permanent demilitarization of the west bank of the Rhine and a strip along the east bank, and for severe limitations upon German land forces, the guarantee treaties afforded such security as the French were determined to achieve.

A second issue, that of reparations and indemnities, evoked perhaps the most protracted debates at the conference and the most lasting bitterness afterward. In cynical disregard of the Pre-Armistice Agreement, which stipulated that Germany should be liable for civilian damages, Clemenceau and Lloyd George demanded that she be made to shoulder the entire costs of the war to the Allied peoples. In the face of an aroused British and French public opinion and heavy pressure by their leaders, Wilson made perhaps his most conspicuous concessions at Paris. First, he agreed that Germany should be forced to bear the costs of disability pensions to Allied veterans and their families, on the ground that these were really civilian damages. Second, he approved the inclusion of Article 231 in the treaty, by which Germany and her allies were forced to accept responsibility for all Allied war losses and damages, although this responsibility was actually limited to civilian damages in Article 232. Third, he agreed that the French should have the right to occupy the Rhineland beyond the stipulated period if the Germans failed to meet their reparations obligations. In addition, the President consented to the immediate Allied seizure of some $5 billion worth of German property; French ownership of the coal mines in the Saar Valley, as compensation for the wanton destruction wrought in France by the retreating German army; and French occupation of the Saar under the supervision of the League of Nations for twenty years.

Actually, the concessions that Wilson made would not have mattered much if he had succeeded in winning the crucial point for which he and his financial advisers fought so hard. It was the proposal that a Reparations Commis-

sion be established to fix a schedule of reparations payments to be made for a definite period, the amount to be
determined, not upon the basis of Allied hopes, but upon
the basis of Germany's capacity to pay. Under the American plan, moreover, the Commission might reduce or
cancel reparations payments altogether if they proved to
be more than the German economy could sustain.

In the controversy that ensued the British were badly
divided, but they finally veered toward the American
position. But on April 5, 1919, just at the time when it
seemed that the American plan might prevail, Colonel
House (speaking for the ailing President) surrendered un-
conditionally to the French demands, by agreeing that the
Reparations Commission should be instructed only to com-
pute the reparations bill and to enforce its complete payment, without any reference to a definite period or to
Germany's capacity to pay. It was a disastrous instance
of yielding, for it bound the President to the French
position and guaranteed that the reparations settlement
would embitter international relations until statesmen
finally admitted that it had been a fiasco from the beginning.

A third issue, one that threatened to disrupt the conference almost before it could begin, was the question of
the disposition of the former German colonies, all of which
had been occupied by Allied forces during the war. In
the Fourteen Points Wilson had called for an " absolutely
impartial adjustment of all colonial claims " with due
regard for the interests of the peoples involved. As he
explained during preconference discussions in London in
December, 1918, what he had in mind was to make the
former German colonies the common property of the
League and to have them governed by small nations under
specific international mandate and supervision. In pressing for this objective, he ran head-on into commitments

for annexation that the British government had made to the dominions and to Japan, and into an absolutely stubborn determination on the part of the latter that these promises should be honored.

The issue was fought out during the opening days of the Paris conference, with Wilson alone arrayed against Lloyd George and the spokemen of the dominions and of Japan. At no time, it is important to note, did the President envisage the return of the disputed colonies to Germany, for he agreed with most experts who accused the Germans of being oppressive and exploitative masters. (This opinion is still held by most specialists in the field of colonial administration.) Wilson, moreover, soon abandoned his plan for mandating the colonies to small nations, on the ground that it was impractical, and accepted the necessity of a division on a basis of occupation. But he refused to yield the chief objective for which he fought, the clear establishment of the principle that the governments to which the former German possessions were awarded should hold those colonies under the specific mandate and supervision of the League for the benefit of the native peoples affected and of the entire world. This was a notable victory, perhaps more notable than Wilson himself realized, because the establishment of the mandate system spelled the eventual doom of colonialism, not merely in the mandates, but throughout the entire world.

Wilson suffered momentary defeat, however, on the closely related issue of Japanese rights in the Shantung Province of China, a matter infinitely more complicated than the disposition of the German colonies because it involved the entire balance of power in the Far East.[16]

---

[16] In writing this and the following paragraph, I have leaned heavily upon the recent excellent study, Russell H. Fifield, *Woodrow Wilson and the Far East, The Diplomacy of the Shantung Question* (New York, 1952).

The Japanese had entered the war in 1914, captured the German naval base at Kiaochow, China, and overrun the entire German concession in the Shantung Province. They had proceeded afterward, from 1915 to 1917, to impose treaties upon the Chinese government recognizing their rights as successors to Germany in the province and to win a similar recognition from the foreign offices in London, Paris, and Petrograd. Legally, therefore, the Japanese claims at the Paris conference were nearly impregnable.

But technical legalities carried little weight with the man who was fighting to help the Chinese people recover a lost province and to avert the danger of Japanese domination of northern China; and with almost incredible effrontery Wilson set out to vindicate the principle of self-determination. He presented the Chinese delegates to the conference, so that they could plead their own case. He appealed to sentiments and principles with unrivaled eloquence, urging the Japanese to make their contribution to a better world by foregoing conquest. Only after it was indelibly clear that the Japanese would sign no treaty that did not recognize their claims did Wilson withdraw his pressure. In agreeing to recognize Japan's right to the former concession, however, the President won verbal promises that full sovereignty in the Shantung Province would be restored to China, a pledge the Japanese later honored.

A fifth issue, the question of Italian claims to former parts of the Austro-Hungarian Empire, provoked the bitterest personal acrimony at the Paris conference. In line with their national traditions, the Italians had bargained astutely with both alliances in 1914 and 1915 and had entered the war against the Central Powers in the latter year under the terms of the Treaty of London, by which the Allies had promised the Italians the Austrian Trentino to the Brenner Pass, the district of Trieste, the Dalmatian coast below the port of Fiume, and other territories.

There would have been no great conflict at Paris over this matter if the Italians had succeeded in keeping their appetites within reasonable bounds. Following the detailed interpretation of the Fourteen Points prepared by Frank Cobb and Walter Lippmann of The Inquiry in October, 1918, Wilson conceded Italy's claim to the Trentino on strategic grounds even before the peace conference opened, although he perhaps later regretted this concession when he realized the degree to which it violated the principle of self-determination. Nor did he object to the Italian claims to Trieste, which were in accord with the Fourteen Points, even though they had been confirmed in the kind of diplomatic bargaining that he detested most.

Conflict between Wilson and the Italian Prime Minister and Foreign Minister, Vittorio Orlando and Sidney Sonnino, arose chiefly because the latter, not satisfied with their more or less legitimate fruits of victory, demanded also the Adriatic port of Fiume, which had been awarded to the South Slavs by the Treaty of London and would be the only good outlet to the sea for the new state of Yugoslavia. By thus overreaching themselves, the Italians alienated their British and French friends and gave Wilson a strategic opportunity that he quickly exploited. In brief, he capitalized upon the weakness of the Italian claim to Fiume to justify a sweeping denial of the Italian right to the Dalmatian coast and, through it, complete control of the Adriatic.

The climax of the grueling battle came on April 23, 1919, when Wilson, sick of making futile pleas to the masters of the old diplomacy, appealed over their heads directly to the Italian people. In a gigantic bluff Orlando and Sonnino left the conference, only to return in early May after it was evident that the President would not yield. There then ensued the most incredible negotiations of the entire conference and a final recognition that the peacemakers could not agree upon the Fiume and Adriatic issues. They were left for settlement by the League of Nations and by direct negotiations between Italy and Yugoslavia.

Four other great issues before the Paris conferees were no less important than the ones we have discussed, but it will serve our purposes here merely to describe the role that Wilson played in helping to find solutions for them.

First, there was the business of redeeming the promise, made by all the belligerents during the war, to establish an independent Poland.[17] The only controversies of any consequence about this matter involved the disposition of the port of Danzig and the German province of Upper Silesia. In both disputes Wilson joined Lloyd George in standing firm against Polish and French demands and in winning the internationalization of Danzig and a plebiscite to determine how Upper Silesia should be partitioned between Germany and Poland.

Second, there was the necessity of deciding the fate of the component remains of the Austro-Hungarian Empire. Wilson's role in this matter has been gravely misunderstood and distorted, especially by certain British critics who have ascribed to him virtually full responsibility for the destruction of the Empire. This is an exaggeration worthy of the good Baron Munchausen. Before the summer of 1918, Wilson had demanded the federalization, not the breaking up, of the realms of the Hapsburgs. Their Empire had already been destroyed from within by centrifugal forces even before Wilson, in the late summer of 1918, specifically amended the Fourteen Points by recog-

[17] See Louis L. Gerson, *Woodrow Wilson and the Rebirth of Poland, 1914–1920* (New Haven, Conn., 1953).

nizing the new state of Czechoslovakia and by thus endorsing the idea of breaking up the Austro-Hungarian Empire. By the time that the Paris Peace Conference assembled the new states of Central Europe existed in fact. They would have been created, and their leaders would have demanded the right of self-determination even though Wilson had never uttered that magic word. All that Wilson or anyone else at Paris, for that matter, could do was to try to draw the least absurd boundary lines possible and to impose arrangements to preserve some degree of economic unity in Central Europe.[18]

Third, there was the even more perplexing necessity of dealing with a chaotic and changing situation in Russia. It is true, as one scholar has recently pointed out, that Wilson's notions about the capacities of the Russian people for effective self-government and self-determination, expressed in Point 6, were romantic.[19] It is also true that he had only a vague understanding of the character of the international communist movement. Yet in spite of it all he arrived intuitively at the right answers, while his Allied conferees, with all their superior knowledge and more " realistic " understanding, arrived at the wrong ones.

In all the inter-Allied discussions about Russia before and during the peace conference, Wilson defended two propositions—first, that the Russian people must be permitted to solve their internal problems without outside intervention, and, second, that communism was a revolutionary answer to egregious wrongs and could be met only by removing its root causes, not by force. As he put it, " In my opinion, trying to stop a revolutionary move-

[18] As Victor S. Mamatey shows in his excellent study, *The United States and East Central Europe, 1914–1918: A Study in Wilsonian Diplomacy and Propaganda* (Princeton, N. J., 1957).

[19] George F. Kennan, *Soviet-American Relations, 1917–1920, Russia Leaves the War,* especially pp. 242-74.

ment by troops in the field is like using a broom to hold back a great ocean." [20]

Wilson acted throughout in accord with these assumptions.[21] During 1918 he resisted heavy Allied pressure for a general anti-Bolshevik intervention. Finally yielding to what seemed to be military and humane necessities, he sent American troops to Archangel and Vladivostok, but only for specific purposes, not for general political intervention in the Russian Civil War, and only in small numbers and for the briefest time possible, as if to chaperone Allied conduct in these areas. At the peace conference, moreover, he again resisted all British and French suggestions for intervention in Russia proper and even refused to send American troops to Vienna to help halt what seemed to be an onrushing Bolshevik tide. The British and particularly the French executed their own far-reaching military interventions at this time and later, to be sure, but Wilson was in no way responsible for these fiascos.

Fourth, there was the issue of disarmament, the key, Wilson believed, to peace and security in the future. What the President proposed was that the victors accept virtually the same limitations that they were imposing upon the Germans, by agreeing in the peace treaty itself to abolish conscription, prohibit private manufacture of the implements of war, and maintain armies sufficient only to preserve domestic order and fulfill international obligations. What Wilson encountered was insuperable oppo-

[20] Paul Mantoux, *Les Délibérations du Conseil des Quatre* (2 vols.; Paris, 1955), I, 55.

[21] On this point I have greatly profited by reading Betty Miller Unterberger, *America's Siberian Expedition, 1918–1920* (Durham, N. C., 1956); by my conversations with Professor Chihiro Hosoya of Tokyo, who is presently working upon a large study of the Japanese intervention in Siberia; and by reading parts of the second volume, as yet unpublished, of Professor Kennan's study of Soviet-American relations.

sition from the French; what he won, only a vague promise to undertake general disarmament in the future. Perhaps because he made so little progress toward the limitation of land forces, he never seriously proposed naval disarmament at the conference.

We come now to the one issue that took precedence over all the others in Wilson's plans and purposes—the question of the League of Nations, which I mention last because it was so pervasively involved in all the discussions at Paris. There were two divergent concepts of what the League should be and do that cast a revealing light upon the motives and objectives of opposing forces at Paris. One was the French concept of a league of victors, which would be used to guarantee French military domination of the Continent. Embodied in a draft presented at the first meeting of the League of Nations Commission on February 3, 1919, the French plan envisaged the creation of an international army and a general staff with startling supranational powers. The other was Wilson's concept of a league of all nations, the vanquished as well as the victors, in short, a universal alliance for the purpose of creating a concert of power, not really a supranational agency, but one depending upon the leadership of the great powers, the co-operation of sovereign states, and the organized opinion of mankind for its effectiveness.

With strong British support Wilson had his way easily enough in the meetings of the commission that drafted the Covenant, or constitution, of the League. The crucial conflicts came during the discussions of the Council of Ten and the Big Four, when the French, Italians, Japanese, and even the British at times relentlessly used the threat of refusing to support Wilson's League as a way of exacting concessions on other issues. Time and again Wilson did retreat, but by thus yielding he won the larger goal, a League of Nations constructed almost exactly as he wanted it, the Covenant of which was firmly embedded in all the treaties signed at Paris.

That Covenant was a treaty binding its signatory members in an alliance of nonaggression and friendship and creating the machinery for international co-operation in many fields and for the prevention of war. The heart of the Covenant was embodied in Article 10, which read as follows:

> The Members of the League undertake to respect and preserve as against external aggression the territorial integrity and existing political independence of all Members of the League. In case of any such aggression or in case of any threat or danger of such aggression the Council shall advise upon the means by which this obligation shall be fulfilled.[22]

The structure erected was the League itself, an international parliament with an Assembly in which all members were represented and an executive Council in which the great powers shared a greater responsibility with a minority of smaller states. In addition, there was a judicial branch—a Permanent Court of International Justice, and an administrative arm—a Secretariat and various commissions charged with responsibility for executing the peace treaties and for promoting international co-operation in economic and social fields. It was, Wilson said when he first presented the Covenant to a full session of the conference, " a living thing . . . , a definite guarantee of peace . . . against the things which have just come near bringing the whole structure of civilization into ruin."

Did Wilson fail at Paris? This is a question that has been asked and answered a thousand times by statesmen

[22] Ray Stannard Baker, *Woodrow Wilson and World Settlement* (3 vols.; Garden City, N. Y., 1922), III, 179.

and scholars since the Versailles Treaty was signed in 1919. It will be asked so long as men remember Woodrow Wilson and the world's first major effort to solve the problem of recurring wars. The answer that one gives depends not only upon the circumstances and mood prevailing at the time it is given, but as well upon the view that one takes of history and of the potentialities and limitations of human endeavor. That is to say, it makes a great deal of difference whether one judges Wilson's work by certain absolute so-called moral standards, or whether one views what he did remembering the obstacles that he faced, the pressures under which he labored, the things that were possible and impossible to achieve at the time, and what would have happened had he not been present at the conference.

I should perhaps begin my own assessment by saying that the Versailles Treaty, measured by the standards that Wilson had enunciated from 1916 to 1919, obviously failed to fulfill entirely the liberal peace program. It was not, as Wilson had demanded in his Peace without Victory speech and implicitly promised in the Fourteen Points, a peace among equals. It was, rather, as the Germans contended then and later, a *diktat* imposed by victors upon a beaten foe. It shouldered Germany with a reparations liability that was both economically difficult to satisfy and politically a source of future international conflict.[23]

---

[23] John Maynard Keynes, in his famous *Economic Consequences of the Peace* (New York, 1920), conclusively proved the utter economic absurdity of the reparations settlement (the Carthaginian peace) to the whole postwar generation of scholars in England and America. It is no longer possible to be quite so dogmatic, for Étienne Mantoux, in *The Carthaginian Peace, or The Economic Consequences of Mr. Keynes,* has proved that Keynes was egregiously wrong in his statistical methods and has demonstrated that German resources were in fact fully adequate to satisfy the reparations requirements of the Versailles Treaty. This position is supported by many economists and by Professor Samuel F. Bemis in his *Diplomatic History of the United*

It satisfied the victors' demands for a division of the enemy's colonies and territories. In several important instances it violated the principle of self-determination. Finally, it was filled with pin pricks, like the provision for the trial of the former German Emperor, that served no purpose except to humiliate the German people. It does not, therefore, require much argument to prove that Wilson failed to win the settlement that he had demanded and that the Allies had promised in the Pre-Armistice Agreement.

To condemn Wilson because he failed in part is, however, to miss the entire moral of the story of Versailles. That moral is a simple one: The Paris peace settlement reveals more clearly than any other episode of the twentieth century the tension between the ideal and the real in history and the truth of the proposition that failure inheres in all human striving. It does not make much sense merely to list Wilson's failures. We can see their meaning only when we understand *why* he failed as he did.

Wilson failed at Paris not because he did not fight with all his mind and strength for the whole of the liberal peace program. Never before in his career had he fought more tenaciously or pleaded more eloquently. Nor did he fail because, as John Maynard Keynes and Harold Nicholson have portrayed him in their unkind caricatures, he was incompetent, uninformed, and " bamboozled " by men

States (New York, 1955 ed.). They point out that Hitler spent vastly more money on rearmament than the German nation would have paid in reparations during the 1930's.

These arguments, actually, are unanswerable, but in a larger sense they are also irrelevant. The question is not whether it was possible for the Germans to continue reparations payments over a long period, but whether they were willing to do so; whether the British and French would attempt to coerce the Germans for a long period if the Germans were not willing to continue voluntary payments; and whether the monetary returns were worth all the international ill will that they provoked. To ask the question this way is, it seems to me, to answer it.

of superior wit and learning.[24] Indeed, after reading the records of the deliberations at Paris one cannot escape the feeling that Wilson was the best informed and on the whole the wisest man among the Big Four.

Wilson failed as he did because his handicaps and the obstacles against which he fought made failure inevitable. In the first place, he had lost most of his strategic advantages by the time that the peace conference opened. German military power, upon which he had relied as a balance against Allied ambitions, was now totally gone. Wilson had no power of coercion over Britain and France, for they were no longer dependent upon American manpower and resources for survival. His only recourse, withdrawal from the conference, would have been utterly fatal to his program. It would have meant inevitably a Carthaginian peace imposed by the French, as the British alone could never have prevented the French from carrying out their plans to destroy Germany. In these circumstances, therefore, compromise was not merely a necessity, but a compelling necessity to avert (from Wilson's point of view) a far worse alternative.

In contrast to the strength of the French were Wilson's other weaknesses. His claim to the right to speak in the name of the American people had been seriously weakened by the election of a Republican Congress in November, 1918, and was denied during the peace conference itself by Republican leaders like Senator Henry Cabot Lodge. In addition, there was the failure of Colonel House, upon whom Wilson had relied as his strong right arm, to support liberal peace ideals during that period of the conference when House was still the President's spokesman. House was so eager for harmony that he was willing to

---

[24] Keynes in his *Economic Consequences of the Peace*, cited in the previous footnote, and Nicholson in *Peacemaking 1919, Being Reminiscences of the Paris Peace Conference* (Boston and New York, 1933).

yield almost any demand and on several crucial occasions seriously undercut and compromised the President.

Another of Wilson's obstacles, namely, the character of his antagonists at Paris, has often been overlooked. Clemenceau, Lloyd George, Orlando, Baron Sonnino, and the Japanese delegates were all tough and resourceful negotiators, masters of the game of diplomacy, quick to seize every advantage that the less experienced American offered.

To overcome such opposition Wilson had at his command the threat of withdrawal, the promise of American support for the right kind of settlement and of leadership in the League of Nations, and the fact that he did speak for liberal groups not only in his own country, but throughout the world as well. These were sources of considerable strength, to be sure, but they were not enough to enable Wilson to impose his own settlement.

In spite of it all Wilson did succeed in winning a settlement that honored more of the Fourteen Points—not to mention the additional thirteen points—than it violated and in large measure vindicated his liberal ideals. There was the restoration of Belgium, the return of Alsace-Lorraine to France, and the creation of an independent Poland with access to the sea. There was the satisfaction of the claims of the Central European and Balkan peoples to self-determination. There was the at least momentary destruction of German military power. Most important, there was the fact that the Paris settlement provided machinery for its own revision through the League of Nations and the hope that the passing of time and American leadership in the League would help to heal the world's wounds and build a future free from fear.

As it turned out, many of Wilson's expectations were fulfilled even though the American people refused to play the part assigned to them. For example, the reparations problem was finally solved in the 1920's in a way not dissimilar from the method that Wilson had proposed. Germany was admitted to the League in 1926, and that organization ceased to be a mere league of victors. Effective naval disarmament was accomplished in 1921 and 1930. Even the great and hitherto elusive goal of land disarmament and the recognition of Germany's right to military equality was being seriously sought by international action in the early 1930's. In brief, the Paris settlement, in spite of its imperfections, did create a new international order that functioned well, relatively speaking. And it failed, not because it was imperfect, but because it was not defended when challenges arose in the 1930's.

Thus I conclude by suggesting that for Woodrow Wilson the Paris Peace Conference was more a time of heroic striving and impressive achievement than of failure. By fighting against odds that would have caused weaker men to surrender, he was able to prevent the Carthaginian kind of peace that we have seen to our regret in our own time; and he was able to create the machinery for the gradual attainment of the kind of settlement that he would have liked to impose at once. The Paris settlement, therefore, was not inevitably a " lost peace." It could have been, rather, the foundation of a viable and secure world order and therefore a lasting memorial to its chief architect, if only the victors had maintained the will to enforce what Wilson signed.

✍

CHAPTER V

WILSON *and the great debate
over collective security*

HAVING HELPED TO LAY the foundations of a new world order in Paris, Wilson returned to the United States in June, 1919, to face the crucial task of winning the approval of the Senate and the support of the people for the Versailles Treaty, the principal part of the Paris settlement.

During the months following Wilson's homecoming, indeed until the election of 1920, there ensued in the United States a debate no less important than the great debate of 1787 to 1789 over the ratification of the Constitution. At stake in the latter-day discussion was the issue of American participation in a new system of collective security. To a large degree the fate of that experiment and the future peace of the world would depend upon the response that the American people gave.

The facts of the treaty fight are well known, so often and in such detail have historians and biographers told the story of the epic parliamentary struggle between Republicans and Democrats and of the bitter personal controversy between the President and his chief antagonist, Senator

Henry Cabot Lodge of Massachusetts. I cannot ignore the forces and factors that cut the channels of the debate and perhaps decisively affected the decisions that the leaders and their followers made. My main purpose in this brief discussion, however, will be to show what has often been obscured by too much concern for dramatic details, namely, the way in which the great debate of 1919-1920 revealed differences in opinion concerning the role that the United States should play in foreign affairs, differences that were fundamental and authentic because they transcended partisanship and personality and have as much relevance for Americans of the mid-twentieth century as they had in Wilson's day.

The lines of battle over ratification of the Treaty of Versailles were first drawn, not after that treaty had been signed, but before Wilson went to Paris, as a consequence of three decisions that he made between October and December of 1918. The first was his decision to issue an appeal to the country on October 25 for the election of a Democratic Congress, and by so doing to make the forthcoming election a specific test of national confidence in his conduct of foreign affairs. The second was his decision to ignore the Senate and the Republican party in discussions of the possible terms of the settlement and in the appointment of the American delegation to the Paris conference, and to name only such men as he thought would be loyal to him and his ideals and subordinate to his direction. The third was Wilson's decision to go to Paris in person, as the head of the American commission.

The first two decisions were certainly egregious mistakes. On the other hand, Wilson was probably right in deciding that he had to go to Paris to take personal leadership in the fight for a liberal peace. However, the important point is not whether Wilson acted wisely or foolishly; it is the way in which his preparations for the peace conference predetermined the shape of the battle over the treaty that would be signed. By appealing for the election of a Democratic Congress on the ground that a Republican victory would imply a repudiation of his leadership in foreign affairs, and by appointing a peace commission composed with one unimportant exception of Democrats, Wilson made a partisan division on the issues of peace inevitable. In other words, he made it certain that Republicans would oppose and Democrats would support whatever treaty he might help to write. Moreover, by first ignoring the Senate in his appointment of the commissioners, and then by going himself to Paris, Wilson made it inevitable that the treaty fight would renew in virulent form the old conflict between the president and the upper house for control of foreign policy.

While Wilson was in Paris there were unmistakable signs at home that he would encounter bitter opposition when he returned with his peace treaty. The most ominous of these was the so-called " Round Robin " resolution that Senator Lodge presented to the upper house on March 4, 1919. Signed by thirty-seven senators, it declared that the Covenant of the League of Nations, " in the form now proposed to the peace conference," was unacceptable. At the same time, frankly isolationist opponents of the League were beginning a furious rhetorical attack in the Senate chamber.

Although there were limits beyond which Wilson would not go in compromise, as he said in a New York address on the eve of his return to France after a brief visit to the United States in late February and early March of 1919, he yielded to the advice of friends who urged him to conciliate his critics. For example, he endeavored to assuage the signers of the " Round Robin " resolution by permitting Henry White. the Republican member of the

American peace delegation, to attempt to ascertain from Lodge why the Covenant was unacceptable to them. Or again, after Lodge had refused to answer specifically, Wilson took the advice of former President William Howard Taft and other Republican supporters of the League and obtained amendments to meet certain American criticisms of the Covenant.[1]

Undertaken reluctantly at best, these measures did little to conciliate the extreme opposition or to conceal Wilson's true feelings about his senatorial critics and his growing determination to defy them. The more he had to concede at Paris during the final months of the conference, the more this determination hardened. By the time he signed the Versailles Treaty, Wilson was obviously sick of making compromises and eager to return to a political arena in which he could fight hard again, without the necessity of giving ground to opponents who had as much power as he. " I have found one can never get anything in this life that is worth while without fighting for it," he told Colonel House, who had urged him to meet the Senate in a conciliatory spirit, on the day that he left Paris.[2]

Arriving in Washington on July 8, the President made no effort to conceal his fighting mood. When a reporter asked him on July 10 whether the Versailles Treaty could be ratified if the Senate added certain reservations, Wilson shot back, " I do not think hypothetical questions are concerned. *The Senate is going to ratify the treaty.*"[3] To cite another example, the French Ambassador, Jules Jusserand,

---

[1] These amendments provided for the right of members of the League to withdraw after giving due notice, exempted domestic questions from the jurisdiction of the League, permitted member nations to refuse to accept a colonial mandate, and accorded formal recognition to the Monroe Doctrine.

[2] Charles Seymour (ed.), *The Intimate Papers of Colonel House* (4 vols.; New York, 1926–1928), IV, 487.

[3] Quoted in Thomas A. Bailey, *Woodrow Wilson and the Great Betrayal* (New York, 1945), p. 9.

went to the White House at about the same time with a
plan that he thought would assure the Senate's approval
of the treaty. Conceived by President Nicholas Murray
Butler of Columbia University and approved by a large
number of Republican senators, this plan envisaged the
adoption of certain reservations to the treaty to protect
American sovereignty and congressional control over the
war-making power. If the President would only accept the
reservations, Jusserand urged, there would be no doubt
about the treaty's fate in the Senate. " Mr. Ambassador,"
Wilson replied, " I shall consent to nothing. The Senate
must take its medicine." [4]

Wilson was, therefore, in the mood of a triumphant
leader presenting his adversaries with a *fait accompli*
when he presented the treaty formally to the Senate on
July 10. He did not refer to the senators, as he had often
done before, as his " colleagues " in the conduct of foreign
relations, nor did he use his favorite phrase " common
counsel " or talk about the necessity of agreement among
reasonable men. On the contrary, after " informing " the
senators that a world settlement had been made, he took
the highest possible ground to urge prompt and unqualified approval of the treaty. The League of Nations, he
exclaimed, was the hope of mankind. " Dare we reject it
and break the heart of the world? " He reiterated the
answer in an impromptu peroration at the end:

> The stage is set, the destiny disclosed. It has come
> about by no plan of our conceiving, but by the hand of
> God who led us into this way. We cannot turn back.
> We can only go forward, with lifted eyes and freshened
> spirit, to follow the vision. It was of this that we

[4] Nicholas Murray Butler, *Across the Busy Years, Recollections and Re-
flections* (2 vols.; New York, 1939–1940), II, 197-201.

dreamed at our birth. America shall in truth show the
way. The light streams upon the path ahead, and no-
where else.[5]

Many historians have been frankly puzzled by Wilson's
refusal even to attempt to build support for the peace
settlement in the Senate and the Republican party—among
the very men who would have the power of life or death
over the Treaty of Versailles. How could an authority on
the American constitutional system have forgotten the
Senate's jealous role in foreign affairs? How could an
intelligent and astute political strategist have done the
things best calculated to assure the defeat of plans upon
which he thought depended the future happiness of mankind? The dilemma inherent in these hyperbolic questions is much more apparent than real. In fact, it is not
too much to say that Wilson acted in the only way that it
was possible for him to act, given his convictions concerning the President's control over foreign relations, his belief
in party responsibility, his view of public opinion, and his
own temperament.

As we have seen in an earlier chapter, Wilson believed
that the president was a virtual sovereign, responsible
only to public opinion and not to Congress, in the conduct
of external affairs.[6] In ignoring the Senate in the appointment of the peace commission, in taking personal responsibility for writing the peace treaty, and in standing de-
fiantly in its defense, he was, therefore, simply playing
the constitutional role that he thought was proper for the
chief executive. Given Wilson's views of party responsibility, moreover, it was inevitable that he should have
ignored the Republican opposition in the processes of
peace-making, because he could not work in harmony with

[5] R. S. Baker and W. E. Dodd, *War and Peace,* I, 548, 551-52.
[6] See above, pp. 22-23.

men whose duty he knew it would be to oppose him at every turn. Given Wilson's urge to dominate and his belief that the Republican leaders, particularly Senator Lodge, represented all the dark forces against which he was battling, it is difficult to imagine him sharing responsibility or dealing with his opponents on a give-and-take basis after his return from Paris.

These are reasons enough to explain the President's methods and his posture of defiance at the beginning of the treaty fight. There was another reason that was more important than all the rest—Wilson's supreme confidence in his own creation and in the overwhelming support of the American people. He knew not only that he was right, but that the people would know that he was right and would crush any man who dared to obstruct the fulfillment of the age-old dream of peace. That was what he meant when he told reporters that of course the Senate would ratify the Versailles Treaty, or when in private he talked about the Senate, that is, the Republican Senate, having to take its medicine.

Actually, the situation was far less simple and reassuring than Wilson imagined at the beginning of the great debate. For one thing, powerful voices were already raised in outright and violent condemnation of the treaty on various grounds. There were the idealists who had thrilled at Wilson's vision of a new world and who now drew back in disgust because the treaty failed to establish a millennial order. There were the so-called hyphenate groups—the German-Americans, who believed that the treaty was a base betrayal of the Fatherland; the Italian-Americans, who were sulking over Wilson's opposition to Italy's demands; and, most important, the several million Irish-Americans, inflamed by the civil war then raging in Ireland, who were up in arms because Wilson had refused to press the cause of Irish independence at Paris and because the treaty allegedly benefited the hated English. There was the powerful chain of Hearst newspapers, marshaling and inciting all the hyphenate protests. There were the out-and-out isolationists, who believed that American membership in the League of Nations would mean entanglement in all of Europe's rivalries and wars. They had powerful advocates in a small group of so-called irreconcilables or bitter-enders in the Senate, led by Hiram Johnson of California, William E. Borah of Idaho, and James A. Reed of Missouri, who opposed the treaty for nationalistic reasons of their own divination.

These were the major groups who opposed ratification of the treaty. In the ensuing debate they were perhaps the loudest and busiest participants of all. They were, however, a minority among the leaders of thought and political opinion, and they spoke for a minority of the people, at least before 1920 if not afterward. This is a simple point but a vital one, because in its important aspects the debate over the treaty was not a struggle between advocates of complete withdrawal on the one side and proponents of total international commitment on the other. It was, rather, a contest between the champions of a strong system of collective security and a group who favored a more limited commitment in international affairs. It was a choice between these alternatives, and not between complete isolation or complete internationalism, that the President, the Senate, and the American people eventually had to make. For this reason, therefore, I propose to let the arguments of the isolationists pass without analyzing them, and to concentrate my attention upon the two main and decisive courses of the debate.

Before we do this, it might be well to remind ourselves of the precise issues at stake. There were differences of opinion in the United States over the territorial and other provisions of the treaty, to be sure, but all of them were insignificant as compared to the differences evoked by the Covenant of the League and its provisions for universal collective security. Those provisions were clear and for the most part unequivocal. There was, of course, Article 10, which guaranteed the political independence and territorial integrity of every member nation throughout the world. There were, besides, Articles 11, 12, 13, 15, 16, and 17, which established the machinery of arbitration for all international disputes susceptible to that procedure and decreed that an act of war against one member nation should " *ipso facto* be deemed to . . . [be] an act of war against all the other Members " and should be followed automatically by an economic blockade against the aggressor and by Council action to determine what military measures should be used to repel the aggression. These were almost ironclad guarantees of mutual security, meant to be effective and unencumbered by the right of any nation involved in a dispute to veto action by the League's Council. Whether such a world-wide system could work, and whether the American people were prepared at this stage of their development to support such a system even if it did—these were the two main issues of the great debate of 1919–1920.

The decisive opposition to the Versailles Treaty came from a group of men who to a varying degree gave negative answers to both these questions. This group included some of the most distinguished leaders in the Senate and out, men like Senator Frank B. Kellogg of Minnesota, Nicholas Murray Butler, former Secretary of State Elihu Root, Charles Evans Hughes, and Herbert Hoover. Most of them were Republicans, because few Democrats active in politics dared to incur the President's wrath by opposing him. They were not isolationists, but limited internationalists who in a varying degree believed that the United States should play an active role in preserving the peace of the world. Most of them favored, for example, arbitration, the establishment of something like a World Court to interpret and codify international law, and international agreements for disarmament, economic co-operation, and the like. Some of them even supported the idea of alliances with certain powers for specific purposes.

On the other hand, all the limited internationalists opposed any such approval of the treaty as would commit the United States unreservedly to such a system of collective security as the Covenant of the League had created. Their arguments might be summarized as follows:

First, a system of collective security that is world-wide in operation is not likely either to work or to endure the strains that will inevitably be put upon it, because in practice the great powers will not accept the limitations that the Covenant places upon their sovereignty, and no nation will go to war to vindicate Article 10 unless its vital interests compel it to do so. Such sweeping guarantees as the Covenant affords are, therefore, worse than no guarantees at all because they offer only an illusory hope of security.

Second, the Covenant's fundamental guarantee, embodied in Article 10, is impossible to maintain because its promise to perpetuate the *status quo* defies the very law of life. As Elihu Root put it:

> If perpetual, it would be an attempt to preserve for all time unchanged the distribution of power and territory made in accordance with the views and exigencies of the Allies in this present juncture of affairs. It would necessarily be futile. . . . It would not only be futile; it would be mischievious. Change and growth are the law of life, and no generation can impose its will in regard to the growth of nations and the distribution of power, upon succeeding generations.[7]

[7] Quoted in Philip C. Jessup, *Elihu Root* (2 vols.; New York, 1938), II, 392-93.

Third, the American people are not ready to support the Covenant's sweeping commitments and in fact should not do so unless their vital interests are involved in a dispute. They would and should be ready to act to prevent the outbreak of any conflict that threatened to lead to a general war, but it is inconceivable that they would or should assume the risk of war to prevent a border dispute in the Balkans, or to help maintain Japanese control of the Shantung Province or British supremacy in Ireland and India. Unconditional ratification of the treaty by the United States would, therefore, be worse than outright rejection, for it would mean the making of promises that the American people could not possibly honor in the future.

Fourth, unqualified membership in the League will raise grave dangers to American interests and the American constitutional system. It will menace American control over immigration and tariff policies, imperil the Monroe Doctrine, increase the power of the president at the expense of Congress, and necessitate the maintenance of a large standing army for the fulfillment of obligations under the Covenant.

Fifth, and most important, full-fledged participation in such a system of collective security as the Covenant establishes will spell the end of American security in foreign affairs, because it will mean transferring the power of decision over questions of peace and war from the president and Congress to an international agency which the United States could not control.

Voicing these objections day in and out as the great debate reached its crescendo in the autumn of 1919, the limited internationalists made their purposes and program indelibly clear. They would accept most of the provisions of the treaty unrelated to the League and acquiesce in the ones that they did not like. They would also sanction

American membership in the League of Nations. But they would also insist upon reserving to the United States, and specifically to Congress, the power of decision concerning the degree of American participation in the League; and they would make no binding promise to enforce collective security anywhere in the future.

This was also the position of Senator Lodge, the man who devised and executed the Republican strategy in the upper house during the parliamentary phase of the treaty struggle. Personally, Lodge had little hope for the success of the League, a profound personal contempt for Wilson, and almost a sardonic scorn for the President's international ideals. The Massachusetts senator was an ardent nationalist, almost a jingoist, no isolationist, but a believer in a strong balance of power. His solution would have been harsh terms, including dismemberment, for Germany and the formation of an Anglo-Franco-American alliance as the best insurance for future peace. But as chairman of the Foreign Relations Committee and leader of his party in the Senate, it was his duty to sublimate his own strong feelings and to find a common ground upon which most Republicans could stand. That common ground, that program acceptable to an overwhelming majority of Republicans inside the Senate and out, was, in brief, to approve the treaty and accept membership in the League, subject to certain amendments and reservations that would achieve the objectives of the limited internationalists.[8]

Debated all through the late summer of 1919, these amendments and reservations were embodied in the report that the Republican majority of the Foreign Relations Committee presented to the upper house on September 10. During the following weeks the Senate rejected the amendments and adopted most of them in the form of reserva-

[8] My understanding of Senator Lodge has been greatly enlarged by reading John A. Garraty, *Henry Cabot Lodge, A Biography* (New York, 1953).

tions, fourteen in all. Most of them were unimportant, but there was one that constituted a virtual rejection of the system of collective security that Wilson had constructed. It was Reservation 2, which declared that the United States assumed no obligations to preserve the territorial integrity or political independence of any other country, unless Congress should by act or joint resolution specifically assume such an obligation. In addition, the preamble to the reservations provided that American ratification of the treaty should not take effect until at least three of the four principal Allied powers had accepted the reservations in a formal exchange of notes.

This, then, was the program to which most of Wilson's opponents stood committed by the time that the Senate moved toward a formal vote on the Versailles Treaty. Whether Lodge himself was an irreconcilable who desired the defeat of the treaty, or whether he was merely a strong reservationist is an important question, but an irrelevant one at this point.[9] The significant fact is that he had succeeded in uniting most Republicans and in commiting them to a program that affirmed limited internationalism at the same time that it repudiated American support of collective security for virtually the entire world.

Meanwhile, despite his earlier show of intransigence, Wilson had been hard at work in preparation for the impending struggle. In an effort to split the Republican ranks, he held a series of conferences in late July with eleven moderate Republican senators who were called mild reservationists because they favored approval of the treaty after the adoption of a few interpretive reservations. On August 19 the President met the Foreign Rela-

[9] For the conflicting points of view on this question, see Denna F. Fleming, *The United States and the League of Nations* (New York, 1932), and T. A. Bailey, *Woodrow Wilson and the Great Betrayal,* previously cited.

tions Committee at the White House for a three-hour grilling on all phases of the settlement. In spite of these overtures, there were unmistakable signs that Wilson had failed to win the support of any large number of Republican senators and that the strong reservationists and isolationists were rapidly gaining ground in the debate that was now proceeding in full fury throughout the country.

In response, Wilson made one of the most fateful decisions of his career. It was, as he put it, to go to the people and purify the wells of public opinion that had been poisoned by the isolationists and opponents of unreserved ratification. He was physically weakened by his labors at Paris, and his physician warned that a long speaking tour might endanger his life. Even so, he insisted upon making the effort to rally the people, the sources of authority, who had always sustained him in the past.

Leaving Washington on September 3, 1919, Wilson headed for the heartland of America, into Ohio, Indiana, Missouri, Iowa, Nebraska, Minnesota, and the Dakotas— into the region where isolationist sentiment was strongest. From there he campaigned through the Northwest and the major cities of the Pacific Coast. The final leg of his journey took him through Nevada, Utah, Wyoming, and Colorado, where the tour ended after Wilson's partial breakdown on September 25 and 26. In all he traveled 8,000 miles in twenty-two days and delivered thirty-two major addresses and eight minor ones. It was not only the greatest speaking effort of Wilson's career, but also one of the most notable forensic accomplishments in American history.

Everywhere that he went Wilson pleaded in good temper, not as a partisan, but as a leader who stood above party strife and advantage. He made his tour, he explained, first of all so that the people might know the truth about the Treaty of Versailles and no longer be confused by the misrepresentations of its enemies. As he put it at Oakland and at Reno:

> One thing has been impressed upon me more than another as I have crossed the continent, and that is that the people of the United States have been singularly and, I some times fear deliberately, misled as to the character and contents of the treaty of peace.

> Some of the critics . . . are looking backward. . . . Their power to divert, or to pervert, the view of this whole thing has made it necessary for me repeatedly on this journey to take the liberty that I am going to take with you to-night, of telling you just what kind of a treaty this is.[10]

In almost every speech, therefore, Wilson explicitly described and defended the major provisions of the treaty and the purposes of its framers. He defended the severity of the articles relating to Germany, on the ground that her crimes against civilization demanded stern punishment. He answered the critics of the Shantung settlement, first by frankly admitting that he did not like the provisions for Japanese control and next by declaring that he had obtained the only possible settlement that offered any hope for China's eventual recovery of the province. In a similar manner he tried to answer other criticisms, and he concluded, not by denying that there were imperfections in the treaty, but by declaring that they were more than counterbalanced by the constructive achievements.

Wilson's supreme purpose was, of course, not to explain the controverted provisions of the treaty relating to territories, colonies, and reparations, but rather to defend the League of Nations against its traducers, to explain the

[10] R. S. Baker and W. E. Dodd, *War and Peace*, II, 265, 327.

system of collective security that its Covenant had established, and to call the American people to the world leadership that he said history now demanded of them.

He began usually by telling how the League of Nations was the fulfillment of an old American dream of peace, how it was an attempt to apply the principles of the Monroe Doctrine to the world at large, how the suggestion of such an organization had come in recent times as much if not more from Republicans than from Democrats, and how he had simply translated American ideas and proposals into statutory form and insisted that they be embodied in the treaty.

The President then proceeded to describe the provisions of the Covenant for collective security, to show how they would work in actual practice, and to attempt to prove that they afforded a system for peace instead of for war. Article 10, he was fond of emphasizing, was the heart of the Covenant and the foundation of the new world order. " Article X," he said at Indianapolis, " speaks the conscience of the world." [11] " Article X," he added at Reno,

is the heart of the enterprise. Article X is the test of the honor and courage and endurance of the world. Article X says that every member of the League, and that means every great fighting power in the world, . . . solemnly engages to respect and preserve as against external aggression the territorial integrity and existing political independence of the other members of the League. If you do that, you have absolutely stopped ambitious and aggressive war . . . , [for] as against external aggression, as against ambition, as against the desire to dominate from without, we all stand together in a common pledge, and that pledge is essential to the peace of the world.[12]

[11] *Ibid.*, I, 610.
[12] *Ibid.*, II, 332-33.

In answer to critics who had argued that unconditional affirmation of Article 10 would involve the United States perpetually in war, Wilson replied by attempting to demonstrate that future wars would be virtually impossible and almost unnecessary if the collective security provisions of the Covenant implementing Article 10 were observed and enforced by the members of the League. To begin with, nations engaged in a dispute that might lead to war were bound to submit their controversy either to arbitration, the World Court, or the Council of the League. Should any nation go to war in violation of these promises, then all the other members of the League would automatically institute a total blockade, "financial, commercial, and personal," against the aggressor.

As Wilson explained at Kansas City:

> We absolutely boycott them [the aggressors]. . . . There shall be no communication even between them and the rest of the world. They shall receive no goods; they shall ship no goods. They shall receive no telegraphic messages; they shall send none. They shall receive no mail; no mail will be received from them. The nationals, the citizens, of the member states will never enter their territory until the matter is adjusted, and their citizens cannot leave their territory. It is the most complete boycott ever conceived in a public document, and I want to say to you with confident prediction that there will be no more fighting after that.[13]

It was possible, of course, Wilson admitted, that war would occur in spite of all these precautions. "Nobody in his senses claims for the Covenant . . . that it is certain to stop war," he said at Indianapolis.[14] If an aggressor flaunted the provisions of the Covenant, and if economic

[13] *Ibid.*, p. 3.
[14] *Ibid.*, I, 613.

measures did not suffice to stop the aggression, then war would probably occur. If it were a major conflagration, then the United States could not remain neutral in any event. If it were a minor controversy far removed from the Western Hemisphere, then the United States would not be directly involved. Enemies of the League had charged that membership in that body would mean American involvement in every dispute everywhere in the world. " If you want to put out a fire in Utah," the President replied at Salt Lake City,

> you do not send to Oklahoma for the fire engine. If you want to put out a fire in the Balkans, if you want to stamp out the smoldering flame in some part of central Europe, you do not send to the United States for troops. The Council of the League selects the powers which are most ready, most available, most suitable, and selects them only at their own consent, so that the United States would in no such circumstances conceivably be drawn in unless the flame spread to the world.[15]

To the charge that membership in the League would impair American sovereignty and require the fulfillment of unpleasant duties, Wilson replied that the contention was, of course, true in part. " The only way in which you can have impartial determinations to this world is by consenting to something you do not want to do," he said at Billings, Montana.

> Every time you have a case in court one or the other of the parties has to consent to do something he does not want to do. . . . Yet we regard that as the foundation of civilization, that we will not fight about these things, and that when we lose in court we will take our medicine.[16]

[15] *Ibid.*, II, 351.
[16] *Ibid.*, pp. 111-12.

It seemed almost superfluous, Wilson added, to argue the necessity of American membership in the League of Nations. There was the obvious fact, he declared at Des Moines, that American isolation had ended,

> not because we chose to go into the politics of the world, but because by the sheer genius of this people and the growth of our power we have become a determining factor in the history of mankind, and after you have become a determining factor you cannot remain isolated, whether you want to or not.[17]

The only question confronting the American people was, therefore, whether they would exercise their influence in the world, which could henceforth be profound and controlling, in partnership with the other powers or in defiance of them. Standing alone, he warned, meant defying the world; defying the world meant maintaining a great standing army and navy; and such militarism and navalism meant the end of democracy at home.

There was the additional fact that without American participation and leadership the League of Nations would become merely another armed alliance instead of a true concert of power. " It would be an alliance," Wilson declared at St. Louis,

> in which the partnership would be between the more powerful European nations and Japan, and the . . . antagonist, the disassociated party, the party standing off to be watched by the alliance, would be the United States of America. There can be no league of nations in the true sense without the partnership of this great people.[18]

[17] *Ibid.*, p. 18.
[18] *Ibid.*, I, 640.

Without American participation and leadership, therefore, the League would fail. Without the League there could be no effective collective security system. Without collective security, wars would come again. American participation was, therefore, essential to peace, the most vital and elemental interest of the United States. This became increasingly the main theme of Wilson's addresses as he journeyed deeper into the West. Over and over he cried out warnings like these:

> Ah, my fellow citizens, do not forget the aching hearts that are behind discussions like this. Do not forget the forlorn homes from which those boys went and to which they never came back. I have it in my heart that if we do not do this great thing now, every woman ought to weep because of the child in her arms. If she has a boy at her breast, she may be sure that when he comes to manhood this terrible task will have to be done once more. Everywhere we go, the train when it stops is surrounded with little children, and I look at them almost with tears in my eyes, because I feel my mission is to save them. These glad youngsters with flags in their hands—I pray God that they may never have to carry that flag upon the battlefield! " [19]

> Why, my fellow citizens, nothing brings a lump into my throat quicker on this journey I am taking than to see the thronging children that are everywhere the first, just out of childish curiosity and glee, no doubt, to crowd up to the train when it stops, because I know that if by any chance we should not win this great fight for the League of Nations it would be their death warrant. They belong to the generation which would then have to fight the final war, and in that final war there would not be merely seven and a half million men slain. The very existence of civilization would be in the balance. . . . Stop for a moment to think about the

[19] At Tacoma, Washington, September 13, 1919, *ibid.*, II, 173.

next war, if there should be one. I do not hesitate to say that the war we have just been through, though it was shot through with terror of every kind, is not to be compared with the war we would have to face next time. . . . Ask any soldier if he wants to go through a hell like that again. The soldiers know what the next war would be. They know what the inventions were that were just about to be used for the absolute destruction of mankind. I am for any kind of insurance against a barbaric reversal of civilization.[20]

Who were the enemies of the League and of the future peace of the world? They were, Wilson declared, the outright isolationists and the men who would destroy the charter of mankind by crippling reservations. They were little Americans, provincials, men of narrow vision. " They are ready to go back to that old and ugly plan of armed nations, of alliances, of watchful jealousies, of rabid antagonisms, of purposes concealed, running by the subtle channels of intrigue through the veins of people who do not dream what poison is being injected into their systems." [21] " When at last in the annals of mankind they are gibbeted, they will regret that the gibbet is so high." [22]

One by one Wilson answered the specific criticisms of the Covenant relating to the Monroe Doctrine, the right of members to withdraw, and the question whether the League had any jurisdiction over the domestic affairs of member nations. He told how he had obtained revision of the Covenant to satisfy American doubts about its first draft. These amendments, he continued, were embodied in the Covenant and were written in language as explicit as he knew how to devise. He would not object to reserva-

[20] At San Diego, California, September 19, and at Denver, Colorado, September 2, 1919, *ibid.*, pp. 291, 391-92.

[21] *Ibid.*, p. 235.

[22] *Ibid.*, p. 9.

tions that merely clarified the American understanding of these questions. Reservations that in any way changed the meaning of the Covenant were, however, more serious, because they would require the re-negotiation of the treaty.

There remained the greatest threat of all to the integrity of the Covenant, the challenge of the Lodge reservations to Article 10. This reservation, Wilson warned, would destroy the foundations of collective security, because it was a notice to the world that the American people would fulfill their obligations only when it suited their purposes to do so. " That," the President exclaimed at Salt Lake City, " is a rejection of the Covenant. That is an absolute refusal to carry any part of the same responsibility that the other members of the League carry." [23] " In other words, my fellow citizens," he added at Cheyenne,

what this proposes is this: That we should make no general promise, but leave the nations associated with us to guess in each instance what we were going to consider ourselves bound to do and what we were not going to consider ourselves bound to do. It is as if you said, " We will not join the League definitely, but we will join it occasionally. We will not promise anything, but from time to time we may coöperate. We will not assume any obligations." . . . This reservation proposes that we should not acknowledge any moral obligation in the matter; that we should stand off and say, " We will see, from time to time; consult us when you get into trouble, and then we will have a debate, and after two or three months we will tell you what we are going to do." The thing is unworthy and ridiculous, and I want to say distinctly that, as I read this, it would change the entire meaning of the treaty and exempt the United States from all responsibility for the preservation of peace. It means the rejection of the treaty, my fellow countrymen, nothing less. It means that the United

[23] *Ibid.*, p. 350.

States would take from under the structure its very foundations and support.[24]

The irony of it all was, Wilson added, that the reservation was actually unnecessary, *if the objective of its framers was merely to reserve the final decision for war to the American government.* In the case of all disputes to which it was not a party, the United States would have an actual veto over the Council's decision for war, because that body could not advise member nations to go to war except by unanimous vote, exclusive of the parties to the dispute. Thus, the President explained, there was absolutely no chance that the United States could be forced into war against its will, unless it was itself guilty of aggression, in which case it would be at war anyway.

These were, Wilson admitted, legal technicalities, and, he added, he would not base his case for American participation in the League of Nations upon them. The issue was not who had the power to make decisions for war, but whether the American people were prepared to go wholeheartedly into the League, determined to support its collective system unreservedly, and willing to make the sacrifices that were necessary to preserve peace. Wilson summarized all his pleading with unrivaled feeling at the Mormon capital, as follows:

> Instead of wishing to ask to stand aside, get the benefits of the League, but share none of its burdens or responsibilities, I for my part want to go in and accept what is offered to us, the leadership of the world. A leadership of what sort, my fellow citizens? Not a leadership that leads men along the lines by which great nations can profit out of weak nations, not an exploiting power, but a liberating power, a power to show the world that when America was born it was indeed a

[24] *Ibid.*, pp. 381-82.

finger pointed toward those lands into which men could deploy some of these days and live in happy freedom, look each other in the eyes as equals, see that no man was put upon, that no people were forced to accept authority which was not of their own choice, and that out of the general generous impulse of the human genius and the human spirit we were lifted along the levels of civilization to days when there should be wars no more, but men should govern themselves in peace and amity and quiet. That is the leadership we said we wanted, and now the world offers it to us. It is inconceivable that we should reject it.[25]

We come now to the well-known tragic sequel. Following his address at Pueblo, Colorado, on September 25, 1919, the President showed such obvious signs of exhaustion that his physician canceled his remaining engagements and sped the presidential train to Washington. On October 2 Wilson suffered a severe stroke and paralysis of the left side of his face and body. For several days his life hung in the balance; then he gradually revived, and by the end of October he was clearly out of danger. But his recovery was only partial at best. His mind remained relatively clear; but he was physically enfeebled, and the disease had wrecked his emotional constitution and aggravated all his more unfortunate personal traits.

Meanwhile, the Senate was nearing the end of its long debate over the Treaty of Versailles. Senator Lodge presented his revised fourteen reservations on behalf of the Foreign Relations Committee to the upper house on November 6, 1919. Senator Gilbert M. Hitchcock of Nebraska, the Democratic minority leader, countered with five reservations, four of which Wilson had approved in substance before he embarked upon his western tour. They simply sought to make clear the American under-

[25] *Ibid.*, p. 355.

standing of Article 10 and other provisions of the treaty. The issue before the Senate was, therefore, now clear— whether to approve the treaty with reservations that did not impair the American obligation to enforce collective security, or whether to approve the treaty with reservations that repudiated all compelling obligations and promised American support for only a limited international system.

Lodge beat down the Hitchcock reservations with the help of the irreconcilables and then won adoption of his own. Now the President had to choose between ratification with the Lodge reservations or running the risk of the outright defeat of the treaty. He gave his decision to Hitchcock in a brief conference at the White House on November 17 and in a letter on the following day: Under no circumstances could he accept the Lodge reservation to Article 10, for it meant nullification of the treaty. When the Senate voted on November 19, therefore, most of the Democrats joined the irreconcilables to defeat ratification with the Lodge reservations by a count of thirty-nine ayes to fifty-five nays. Hoping to split the Republican ranks and win the support of the " mild reservationists," the Democratic leaders then moved unconditional approval of the treaty. This strategy, upon which Wilson had placed all his hopes, failed, as a firm Republican majority defeated the resolution with the help of the irreconcilables by a vote of thirty-eight ayes to fifty-three nays.

It was not the end, for during the following months an overwhelming majority of the leaders of opinion in the United States refused to accept the Senate's vote as the final verdict. In the absence of any reliable indices, it is impossible to measure the division of public opinion as a whole; but there can be little doubt that an overwhelming majority of thoughtful people favored ratification with some kind of reservations, and even with the Lodge reservations, if that were necessary to obtain the Senate's consent.

There was, consequently, enormous pressure upon the leaders in both parties for compromise during the last weeks of 1919 and the early months of 1920. Prominent Republicans who had taken leadership in a nonpartisan campaign for the League, including former President Taft and President A. Lawrence Lowell of Harvard University; scores of editors and the spokesmen of various academic, religious, and labor organizations; and Democratic leaders who dared oppose the President, like William J. Bryan and Colonel House, begged Lodge and Wilson to find a common ground. Alarmed by the possibility of American rejection of the treaty, spokesmen for the British government declared publicly that limited American participation in the League would be better than no participation at all.

Under this pressure the moderate leaders in both camps set to work in late December and early January to find a basis for agreement. Even Lodge began to weaken and joined the bipartisan conferees who were attempting to work out an acceptable reservation to Article 10. But the Massachusetts senator and his friends would not yield the essence of their reservation, and it was Wilson who had to make the final choice. By January he had recovered sufficient physical strength to manage his forces in the upper house. All the while, however, his intransigence had been compounded by personal bitterness and by the growing conviction that rejection of the treaty was preferable to a dishonorable ratification. Consequently, between January and March, 1920, when the final debates and maneuvers were in progress, he rejected all suggestions of yielding on Article 10. Instead, he apparently began to make fantastic plans to run again for the presidency in a campaign that would decide the fate of the treaty. " If there is any doubt as to what the people of the country think on this vital matter," he wrote in a letter to the Democratic party on January 8, 1920, " the clear and single way out is to submit it for determination at the next election to the voters of the Nation, to give the next election the form of a great and solemn referendum."

Thus the parliamentary phase of the struggle moved to its inexorable conclusion when the Senate took its second and final vote on the treaty on March 19, 1920. The only hope for approval lay in the chance that enough Democrats would defy the President, as many friends of the League were urging them to do, to obtain a two-thirds majority for ratification with the Lodge reservations. Twenty-one Democrats did follow their consciences rather than the command from the White House, but not enough of them defected to put the treaty across. The treaty with the Lodge reservations failed by seven votes.

There was a final sequel. The Democratic presidential and vice-presidential candidates, James M. Cox and Franklin D. Roosevelt, tried hard to make the election of 1920 a " great and solemn referendum " on the League. But the effort failed, because so many other issues were involved, because the Republican candidate, Warren G. Harding, equivocated so artfully that no one knew where he stood, and because virtually all the distinguished leaders of the G. O. P. assured the country that a Republican victory promised the best hope of American membership in the League. These promises were obviously not honored. One of the new President's first official acts was to repudiate the idea of membership in the League; one of the new administration's first foreign policies was to conclude a separate peace with Germany.

Virtually all historians now agree that Wilson's refusal to permit his followers in the Senate to approve the treaty with the Lodge reservations was an error of tragic magnitude. Having built so grandly at Paris, having fought so magnificently at home for his creation, he then proceeded by his own hand to remove the cornerstone of his edifice of peace. Why? Were there inner demons of pride and arrogance driving him to what one historian has called " the supreme infanticide "? Did his illness and seclusion prevent him from obtaining a realistic view of the parliamentary situation, or so disarrange him emotionally that he became incompetent in the tasks of statesmanship? Or was he simply an idealist who would make no compromises on what he thought were fundamental principles?

The historian, who sees through a glass darkly when probing the recesses of the mind, is not able to give final answers to questions like these. Wilson, for all his high-mindedness and nobility of character, was headstrong and not much given to dealing graciously or to compromising with men whom he distrusted and disliked. Once before, in a violent dispute at Princeton over control of the graduate school, he had revealed these same traits and suffered defeat because he could not work with men whom he did not trust. The sympathetic biographer would like to believe that it was his illness, which aggravated his bitterness and his sense of self-righteousness, that drove Wilson to his fatal choice. Perhaps this is true. He had not always been incapable of compromise; perhaps he would have yielded in the end if disease had not dethroned his reason.

These attempts to extenuate ignore the fact that there were fundamental and vital issues at stake in the controversy over the treaty—whether the United States would take leadership in the League of Nations without hesitations and reservations, or whether it would join the League grudgingly and with no promises to help maintain universal collective security. To Wilson the difference between what he fought for and what Lodge and the Republicans would agree to was the difference between the success or failure and the life or death of man's best hope for peace. This he had said on his western tour, at a time when his health and reasoning faculties were unimpaired. This he believed with his heart and soul. It is, therefore, possible, even probable, that Wilson would have acted as he did even had he not suffered his breakdown, for it was not in his nature to compromise away the principles in which he believed.

If this is true, then in this, the last and greatest effort of his life, Wilson spurned the role of statesman for what he must have thought was the nobler role of prophet. The truth is that the American people were not prepared in 1920 to assume the world leadership that Wilson offered them, and that the powers of the world were not yet ready to enforce the world-wide, universal system of collective security that the President had created.

Collective security failed in the portentous tests of the 1930's, not because the League's machinery was defective, but because the people of the world, not merely the American people alone, were unwilling to confront aggressors with the threat of war. As a result a second and more terrible world conflict came, as Wilson prophesied it would, and at its end the United States helped to build a new and different league of nations and took the kind of international leadership that Wilson had called for. But events of the past decade have not fully justified Wilson's confidence in international organization; the only really promising systems of collective security, the regional ones like NATO, have been of a kind that Wilson fervently denounced; and only the future can reveal whether his dream of a universal system can ever be made a reality.[26]

[26] For a provocative reply in the negative, see Robert E. Osgood, " Woodrow Wilson, Collective Security, and the Lessons of History," *Confluence,* v (Winter, 1957), 341-54.

And so it was Wilson the prophet, demanding greater commitment, sacrifice, and idealism than the people could give, who was defeated in 1920. It is also Wilson the prophet who survives in history, in the hopes and aspirations of mankind and in whatever ideals of international service that the American people still cherish. One thing is certain, now that men have the power to sear virtually the entire face of the earth: The prophet of 1919 was right in his larger vision; the challenge that he raised then is today no less real and no less urgent than it was in his own time.

INDEX

INDEX

✒

Adams, John Quincy, 9.

Alsace-Lorraine: factor in causing World War, 33; return of to France an Allied war aim, 64; return of to France suggested by Wilson in Fourteen Points address, 103; awarded to France by Versailles Treaty, 124.

American Socialist Party, 92.

Anglo-American relations: early American response to British maritime system, 36–39; controlling factors in British maritime policies, 39–40; American acceptance of British maritime measures, 40–43; growth of war trade and lifting of American ban on loans, 43–46; negotiation of House-Grey Agreement and beginning of Wilson's mediation efforts, 46–51; impact on Wilson during armed ship and *Sussex* crises, 57–59; failure of mediation under House-Grey Agreement, 62–67; deterioration of during summer and autumn of 1916, 67–70; British consent to Wilson's mediation, 72–73; relations during war, 97–98; 101; and armistice negotiations, 108; British spokesmen urge ratification of Versailles Treaty, 152. *See also* Lloyd George, David.

Arabic crisis, 56–57.

Armed ship controversy: *see* German-American relations.

Armed ship controversy in Congress, 28.

Article 10 of Covenant of League of Nations: text, 120; criticisms of, 136; " the heart of the enterprise," 142–143; Lodge reservation to denounced by Wilson, 148–149; Wilson-Hitchcock reservation to, 150–151; efforts at compromise over, 152.

Article 231 of Treaty of Versailles, 111.

Assembly of League of Nations, 120.

Austria-Hungary: Wilson's pressure on for withdrawal from war, 98; Wilson suggests autonomy for subject peoples of, 103; Italian demands for former territory of, 114; disintegration and disposal of at Paris Peace Conference, 116–117.

Balance of power: as factor in Wilson's decision for war, 88–89; in Far East, 113–114.

Balfour, Arthur, 97.

Belgium: Wilson's attitude toward atrocities in, 35; Wilson refuses to protest German violation of, 51; restoration of an Allied war aim, 64; German " promise " to evacu-

159

marine issue, 80–81; breaks relations with Germany, 82; announces acceptance of submarine blockade under conditions, 82–84; requests permission for armed neutrality, 84–85; arms merchantmen, 85; accepts decision for war, 85–90; takes leadership in liberal peace program, 94; announces readiness of United States to join League of Nations, 95; joins liberal peace program to League concept, 96–97; defines America's role in World War, 97–98; begins campaign for liberal peace in 1917, 98–100; responds to Pope's peace appeal, 100–101; fails to persuade Allies to approve liberal peace pronouncement, 101; delivers Fourteen Points address, 102–104; discusses peace program with Austrians and Germans, 104–105; enunciates Four Supplementary Points, 105; reaction to Treaty of Brest-Litovsk, 105–106; announces Four Additional Points, 107n; conducts armistice negotiations, 107–108; and problem of French security at Paris Peace Conference, 109–111; signs security treaty with France, 110–111; and struggle over reparations settlement, 111–112; and colonial settlement, 112–113; and Italian territorial claims, 115–116; and re-establishment of Poland, 116; role in dismemberment of Austria-Hungary, 116–117; and question of intervention in Russia, 117–118; wins establishment of League of Nations, 119–120; failures at Paris, 120–124; accomplishments at Paris, 124–125; issues call for election of Democratic Congress, 128–129; ignores Senate and Republicans in selecting Peace Commission, 128–

129; decides to go to Paris, 128–129; attempts to satisfy critics of Versailles Treaty, 129–130; in fighting mood upon return from Paris, 130–131, 132–133; presents Treaty to Senate, 131–132; attempts to win Republican support, 139–140; undertakes western tour to arouse support for Treaty, 140; explains Treaty, 140–141; defends League, Article 10, and collective security system, 141–144; says American leadership in League essential to prevention of second World War, 145–147; denounces enemies of League, 147; explains revision of Covenant and position on reservations, 147–148; denounces Lodge reservation to Article 10, 148–149; appeals for American international leadership, 149–150; breakdown, 150; refuses to accept Lodge reservations before first Senate vote, 151; refuses any compromise, declares election of 1920 will be "great and solemn referendum" on League, 152–153; reasons for refusal to compromise, 153–155; as prophet, 155–156.

Wiseman, Sir William, 72.

Woman's Peace Party of the United States, 93.

World Court, 120, 136, 143.

World War I: American attitudes toward, 32–33, 66, 68; fateful turning point in, 61; military developments in autumn of 1916, 74; military developments from March to October 1918, 106–107.

Yugoslavia: awarded Fiume by Treaty of London, 115; settlement of Fiume issue with Italy, 116.

Zimmermann telegram, 89.